Spotlight on Your Inclusive Classroom

A teacher's toolkit of instant inclusive activities

Glynis Hannell

 Routledge
Taylor & Francis Group

LONDON AND NEW YORK

First published 2009
by Routledge
2 Park Square, Milton Park, Abingdon, Oxon OX14 4RN

Routledge is an imprint of the Taylor & Francis Group, an informa business

© 2009 Glynis Hannell

Typeset in Sabon by
Florence Production Ltd, Stoodleigh, Devon
Printed and bound in Great Britain by
MPG Books Ltd, Bodmin

British Library Cataloguing in Publication Data
A catalogue record for this book is available from the British Library

ISBN10: 0–415–47306–3 (pbk)
ISBN13: 978–0–415–47306–4 (pbk)

Contents

Other books from Routledge by Glynis Hannell

Spotlight on Language: A teacher's toolkit of instant language activities
978–0–415–47311–8

Spotlight on Writing: A teacher's toolkit of instant writing activities
978–0–415–47308–8

Spotlight on Reading: A teacher's toolkit of instant reading activities
978–0–415–47307–1

Spotlight on Spelling: A teacher's toolkit of instant spelling activities
978–0–415–47305–7

Success with Inclusion: 1001 Teaching strategies and activities that really work
978–0–415–44534–4

Dyscalculia: Action plans for successful learning in mathematics
978–1–84312–387–3

Dyslexia: Action plans for successful learning
978–1–84312–214–2

Promoting Positive Thinking: Building children's self-esteem, self-confidence and optimism
978–1–84312–257–9

CHAPTER 1

Introduction

Spotlight on everything

Pupils come to the classroom with a wide range of varying experiences, background knowledge and levels of understanding. Teachers, of course, strive to offer every pupil opportunities to maximise their own potential. In doing this teachers have to counteract the disadvantages that some pupils experience through individual differences, special needs, or impoverished cultural and social backgrounds.

Teachers can make a significant impact by providing activities that offer all pupils inclusive, explicit teaching, a range of challenges and exposure to a wide knowledge base.

The Spotlight series of books contain a range of inclusive activities for instant use in the classroom. The other four books in the series focus on four specific areas of learning (Language, Writing, Spelling and Reading).

In contrast, *Spotlight on Your Inclusive Classroom* offers teachers an interesting miscellany of topics and activities, to stimulate, engage, challenge, entertain and extend all the pupils in the class. The activities are quick and interesting to do, and are designed to extend your pupils' thinking skills and knowledge base. They allow the busy teacher to give any group of pupils an inclusive activity in which everyone can participate and learn.

Foundations of success

Words and language

Good language skills equip your pupils to interact on an equal footing within the classroom and community. *Spotlight on Language*, a companion book in this series, is full of intriguing and practical language activities. In Chapter 2 of *Spotlight on Your Inclusive Classroom*, teachers are given additional activities to promote good language skills.

Pupils who have poorly developed language skills are at a significant disadvantage in most areas of life. Imagine being in a foreign country with a poor grasp of the language; just think how isolating and demeaning this would be! The more we understand the language that surrounds us, the more we understand our community and feel able to participate.

Chapter 2 offers a range of language-related activities that will help to develop your pupils' understanding of spoken and written language.

Mathematics

Agility with the language and concepts of mathematics is of course an important part of every child's repertoire. While this book is not intended as a mathematics course book, the activities provided do help to enhance your pupils' mathematical skills.

Chapter 3 provides activities in estimating, working with the calendar, performing basic number operations and simply thinking about numbers. All the activities will contribute to your pupils' competence with mathematics. Many of the items can be treated as oral, classroom activities to encourage lively discussion and brainstorming between pupils of varying abilities.

General knowledge, science and social understanding

Some pupils enjoy the advantage of a home where there are many opportunities for learning about the world around us. Other pupils may be disadvantaged by narrow, limited learning opportunities at home.

Still more pupils, because of their own difficulties with learning, may simply not develop a curiosity. They may remain unaware of all the interesting and useful information in their surroundings.

Chapter 4 of this book, 'The world around us', provides a selection of activities designed to stimulate and fascinate your pupils.

Riddles, jokes and puzzles

We all enjoy riddles, jokes and puzzles! These activities often rely on wordplays, lateral thinking and creativity. As a result they can have real educational value in developing lateral thinking and language skills.

Chapter 5 provides a range of brain-teasers for your pupils to enjoy. These are ideal to fill in a few moments in the busy school day, when there is not enough time to start any new activity.

Effective, inclusive teaching

Let us briefly look at some of the key elements of effective, inclusive teaching:

- Teacher and pupils talk, explore, discuss and work on learning together.

- There are lots of opportunities for pupils to learn from each other.

- The teacher provides individual assistance when pupils need this.

- Every pupil can participate in the same type of activity.

- Classroom activities are individualised to meet pupils' differing skill levels.

- Extra support and scaffolding are given when pupils need them.

- Stereotypes do not limit individual pupils' opportunities.

- All pupils have the chance to take on new challenges and extend themselves.

- Pupils are taught how to think about questions.

- Pupils are taught learning strategies.

- Sub-skills of thinking and learning are taught to all pupils.

- Teaching is explicit and focused.

- Understanding is developed through examples, discussion and explanation.

- All pupils have sufficient practice to master what they have been taught.

- Mistakes or incorrect answers are viewed as valuable teaching opportunities.

- Activities engage the pupils' interest.

- Activities offer disadvantaged pupils enrichment as well as skills.

Spotlight on Your Inclusive Classroom

Differentiated learning materials for inclusion

Each of the activities in this book is presented at three levels of difficulty. Level 1 is the easiest level, Level 2 intermediate and Level 3 the most difficult. There is deliberate overlap between the three levels to allow for easy transition between one level and the next.

One activity can be used to suit a wide range of pupils within a mixed ability class. For example, a teacher may use Level 2 for most of the class, but direct the more able pupils to continue on with Level 3 items, while their younger or less able classmates work on Level 1 items. All pupils will be doing exactly the same activity, but at different levels of difficulty.

The gradual increase in difficulty levels and the overlap between levels helps teachers to provide *differentiated learning materials* in their *inclusive* classrooms.

Pupils with learning difficulties

The graded difficulty levels within each activity allow the teacher to allocate appropriate *differentiated* tasks to a wide range of pupils, so that everyone can be included in the same activity, at varying levels, according to their ability.

Pupils who experience difficulty with language and/or learning may benefit from introductory work on an easier level than some other pupils. This is often sufficient to prepare them to cope with the more *challenging* items that follow. The teacher can make a decision on whether to:

- provide additional teaching support to help the pupil complete the activity; or

- if the first level is successfully completed, have the pupil progress to the more difficult levels of the same activity; or

- if the first level has been completed only with assistance, move the pupil to a similar activity, but at the same level of difficulty as before, and provide assistance as required on the new activity.

For example, Ava and Adam have both completed the first level of *Idioms* (Activity 7). Ava coped with this quite easily so the teacher decides that she should stay with *Idioms* but can now move on to the more challenging second level of this activity.

Adam, however, clearly found Level 1 of *Idioms* quite difficult, so he is not yet ready for the more difficult levels that follow. Instead, the teacher moves Adam 'sideways' to Level 1 of *Proverbs* (Activity 8), which also deals with the interpretation of indirect meaning. In addition, the teacher gives Adam more support and one-to-one assistance so that he copes with Level 1 of *Proverbs* successfully. Adam, therefore, has fresh learning materials and a further opportunity to work with language, but without placing him in a situation where the level of difficulty is too hard for him.

Throughout the book teachers will find opportunities to provide additional input and assistance when this is needed.

A key principle for inclusive teaching is that teachers vary the amount and style of support given to pupils of varying abilities. Many pupils will need extra s*caffolding, support* and *practice* in specific areas of the curriculum. Other pupils may need extra assistance right across all areas. For example, while one pupil may be able to answer a question without any prompts or hints, another may need the teacher to give more scaffolding and assistance such as:

- discussion

- leading questions

- helpful comments, hints or clues

- multiple-choice options.

The resultant learning is still valid, but has required more structure to achieve the end result. For example, Jordan is not sure what the letters UFO stand for in *Acronyms* (Activity 25). His teacher tells him, '*Here's a clue; the FO might stand for Flying Object or it might stand for Flying Orange; which shall we go for?*'

Many of the activities in this book offer multiple-choice answers. This not only provides support for pupils, but also gives the teacher an opportunity to coach pupils in thinking skills. For example, working on the questions in *Do you know?* (Activity 16), a pupil says that cars have number plates '*So you know which car is yours.*' The teacher says '*Yes, that's right*' but adds '*What about other people's point of view? Does your car number help them in any way?*' Learning to think about a situation from another person's viewpoint is an important part of skilled, flexible thinking.

Pupils with advanced development

Pupils who have advanced development usually thrive on activities that *challenge* them, but at the same time enjoy being *included* in the class activity. Teachers can readily select a range of activities and/or levels to provide the bright pupil with tasks that will extend their skills. For example, a very advanced six-year-old might start with Level 2 of the selected activity and even move through to Level 3 if able to do so.

The open *discussion* topics taken from the more difficult levels can be used to promote the advanced pupil's thinking and language skills. The pupil might discuss topics with an adult, or with other bright pupils. The more closed questions can be used to extend the pupil's language, with the teacher giving *guidance, scaffolding* and *support* as required.

Interactive, inclusive and explicit teaching

The activities in this book have all been written so that they can be used as *interactive, inclusive oral activities*. Talking and discussing will therefore play an important role in engaging your pupils in the various activities.

The activities vary in the way they can be handled. For example, in some activities the teacher will ask the pupils closed questions that require very specific responses, such as in *All about animals* (Activity 15). This often leads to pupils researching answers combined with *explicit* teaching, because there are definite *right* or *wrong* answers. However, *discussion* is also often generated and the interplay of ideas between teacher and pupils can provide valuable, *inclusive* and *interactive* learning.

Teachers can also demonstrate and teach good problem-solving strategies, such as '*Well, that one has got me! I'm really not sure where a wombat sleeps. How can we find out?*' Recognising when you don't know an answer, and then using good strategies to find out, is a very important aspect of learning. For pupils who are passive in the face of difficulties this is a very important lesson.

Some activities offer considerable scope for discussion and open-ended answers. For example, *Same and different* (Activity 5) gets you and your pupils engaged in inclusive, interactive discussions. Teachers may sometimes be pleasantly surprised at how some pupils break existing *stereotypes* of what is expected of them in the ways that they deal with these questions.

Other activities, such as those in Chapter 4, 'The world around us', not only develop language skills, but also provide opportunities for inclusive classroom discussion on topics relating to social issues, general knowledge and practical common sense, involving all pupils making their own unique contributions to the group activity. This generates a shared knowledge and understanding that is of real value in helping all children to experience a sense of belonging to their peer group and indeed their wider community. Teachers may also find that this type of work filters back to the children's homes and makes a positive connection between home and school learning.

Teachers are encouraged to use the activities as the basis for inclusive classroom discussions, which may range across various topics, stimulated by the activities in the book. Again these open-ended topics offer many opportunities for teachers to follow through with further development, perhaps in written work or in drama.

User's guide to *Spotlight on Your Inclusive Classroom*

Ethical and inclusive teaching

All the activities in this book have been carefully written to provide teachers with ethical, responsible and inclusive teaching materials. The items promote social responsibility, personal resourcefulness and thoughtfulness towards others.

References to popular culture (such as superheroes or fantasy), the supernatural, specific religious beliefs or inappropriate role models have been avoided.

Flexibility

Teachers can draw activities from any chapter, in any order, according to the needs of a particular group of pupils. All the activities are intended to stimulate and inform your pupils.

Ease and speed of use

The book is ready for instant use in class oral work. The only preparation required is for the teacher to preselect the appropriate activity for the class, group or individual.

The activities provide a variety of valuable learning experiences that can form the basis of a single lesson or series of lessons.

Many activities are also perfect for a quick, intensive burst of group activity, perhaps to settle the class down or fill in a few minutes before the next lesson.

Teaching notes

The teaching notes at the start of each activity provide teachers with a brief rationale for the activity and practical teaching hints. In some situations suggested correct answers, sample answers and guides are provided for the teacher's convenience.

Suitability for parents or teaching assistants

Teachers may find that parents will welcome the activities in this book for fun-based learning at home. Teaching notes also enable paraprofessionals or even volunteers (such as parents assisting in a learning support programme) to use the activities designated by the pupil's teacher.

Suitability for classroom, small group or individual lessons

The activities in this book all lend themselves to small group or individual lessons, in which pupils and teacher work on the items collaboratively. The varied nature of the activities in this book allows teachers to select activities that can form the basis of an individualised programme for a particular pupil or group of pupils with special needs.

All the activities are intended to provide pupils with explicit teaching. As such, they are suitable for pupils with special needs as well as mainstream pupils. The teacher can adjust the degree of individual guidance and support according to the needs of the pupils he or she is working with.

Supplementing a remedial or speech therapy programme

While this book is not intended to provide a special education programme, many of the activities will help to promote the intellectual development of special needs pupils. Every activity is divided into three levels of increasing difficulty, so that a teacher can differentiate the tasks given to pupils according to their individual needs. The book can therefore support pupils who are disadvantaged in various ways.

Worksheets

Many of the activities work very well as oral classroom activities. However, the activities can also be used as written language exercises if required. Teachers are given permission to copy any activity for use with the pupils they teach.

Teachers can identify different levels of difficulty, or different volumes of work. For instance, one pupil might be asked to attempt only Level 1, or the teacher might circle the specific items in an activity that the pupil is required to complete. Alternatively, the teacher may set a given number of items to be completed, for example 'Choose any six questions from this sheet.'

Teachers of pupils with special needs may find it useful to work through the activity with the pupil on one worksheet and then use a clean copy of the worksheet for the pupil to work through the same task again independently.

Making connections

All learning works best if it is connected with other learning. The exchange and cross-fertilisation of emerging skills that occur within a classroom can create a powerful network of interlinked learning.

Teachers will find that they can create links between the activities in this book with other reading, spelling, written language, science and mathematics activities that occur within the classroom.

Follow-on activities

Many teachers will find it useful to devise other, similar activities involving current classroom topics, using the activities in this book as a model. For instance, starting with the activity of *Calendar* (Activity 10), the teacher might then set the pupils further calendar-related activities to build their skills.

Approximate age levels

There are no hard and fast rules about which level of activities should be given to children of a particular age. The activities are flexible and open to teachers to use in a variety of ways with a wide range of ages and abilities. Teachers will be able to make their own decisions about particular activities, based on their knowledge of their pupils' abilities and areas of difficulty.

CHAPTER 2

Words, words, words

Words as building blocks

Words are the building blocks of communication. Without good communication skills your pupils will be disadvantaged in many aspects of their lives. Learning a language is a lifelong process, in which new words, new idioms and different ways of using language can surprise and delight even the oldest learner.

Many pupils with learning difficulties experience frustrations with language skills. They may have a limited vocabulary, or find it difficult to express themselves. Perhaps they find anything other than very concrete language difficult to interpret. Other pupils may have good potential to develop their language skills, but may be held back by social or cultural factors.

One of the companion books to this book is called *Spotlight on Language* and is specifically targeted towards language skills. It contains a wealth of language-related activities that teachers will find invaluable. However, the two books (*Spotlight on Your Inclusive Classroom* and *Spotlight on Language*) can easily be used in conjunction with each other.

Vocabulary is an important part of language and in this chapter there are several activities that extend the pupils' word knowledge. For example, *What do they do?* (Activity 2) teaches the names of occupations, *Synonyms* (Activity 4) teaches, as its name suggests, words that share the same meaning and *Animal babies and groups* (Activity 3) helps pupils to target the correct word.

Two activities are focused on indirect meaning. Many pupils find it difficult to move away from a literal interpretation of what is said. For example, if they are told '*Pull up your socks*' they may, quite literally, adjust their footwear, and not understand that this saying means to try harder in quite another way!

This chapter has two activities that give pupils opportunities to move away from the literal and to work with indirect meaning. *Idioms* (Activity 7) uses a range of commonly used idioms, which can form the basis of interesting classroom discussions. *Proverbs* (Activity 8) introduces pupils to commonly used proverbs, which not only gives valuable learning in language, but also allows the teacher to introduce discussion of ethical and social issues. For example, does the proverb *A bad workman blames his tools* sometimes apply in the classroom? Or how does *Two heads are better than one* or *Waste not, want not* translate into the way the pupils go about their learning in the classroom?

Activity 1: What is it?

Teaching notes

This activity is a vocabulary builder that will help all your pupils to develop a stronger understanding of word meanings. Explicit teaching of words helps to compensate for disadvantages that some pupils have with language. The activity may also stimulate your pupils to be more interested in word meanings. A choice of three possible answers also helps to develop logical thinking, as a pupil may be able to work out the meaning of a word by logical deduction and a process of elimination.

Important note: Teachers should *read* all the items to the pupils. This is essential because the words used will be beyond the reading levels of many of the pupils.

Level 1

1 **b** a fish

2 **a** a type of metal

3 **c** a deep hole in the ground

4 **a** a large spider

5 **a** a large animal

6 **c** an illness you can catch

7 **a** a jewel

8 **c** a type of dog

9 **c** a flower that grows from a bulb

Level 2

1 **b** a bird of prey

2 **c** an instrument to tell direction

3 **a** a small bay on the coast

4 **a** an animal

5 **c** part of your body

6 **a** an instrument that measures heat

7 **b** a place in South America

8 **c** a language spoken by some Chinese people

9 **a** a vegetable with tough leaves

Level 3

1 **c** a heavy book

2 **c** an animal with a hump

3 **a** an animal like a newt

4 **a** a country in Africa

5 **c** part of the eye

6 **a** a purple colour

7 **b** a deep valley between cliffs

8 **b** a type of root vegetable

9 **c** a competition for cowboys

Activity 1

What is it?

Choose the right answer.

LEVEL 1

1 trout   **a** a tool for smoothing wood
    b a fish
    c a pig's nose

2 bronze   **a** a type of metal
    b a musical instrument
    c a loud noise

3 crater   **a** something you cut cheese with
    b a wooden box
    c a deep hole in the ground

4 tarantula   **a** a large spider
    b a crazy dance
    c a sort of meat

5 bison   **a** a large animal
    b a muscle in your arm
    c a sort of bicycle

6 influenza   **a** a light curtain
    b a sort of writing
    c an illness you can catch

7 emerald   **a** a jewel
    b an important man
    c a sort of hat

8 spaniel   **a** someone from Spain
    b a tool that helps mend cars
    c a type of dog

9 tulip   **a** a sort of lipstick
    b a toy for a dog
    c a flower that grows from a bulb

Activity 1

What is it?

Choose the right answer.

LEVEL 2

1 falcon   **a** a thing that helps to light a fire
                 b a bird of prey
                 c a type of knife

2 compass   **a** a sort of boot
                 b a way through the mountains
                 c an instrument to tell direction

3 cove   **a** a small bay on the coast
                 b a small window
                 c a secret message

4 armadillo   **a** an animal
                 b a strap you put on your arm when it is broken
                 c a small group of soldiers

5 tendon   **a** a large tent
                 b a group of ten people
                 c part of your body

6 thermometer   **a** an instrument that measures heat
                 b an instrument that measures if you are sick
                 c an instrument that measures gravity

7 Peru   **a** a sort of warm wool
                 b a place in South America
                 c an animal a bit like a goat

8 Cantonese   **a** a sort of frying pan
                 b a vegetable a bit like broccoli
                 c a language spoken by some Chinese people

9 artichoke   **a** a vegetable with tough leaves
                 b a move in judo
                 c a sword used in olden days

Activity 1

What is it?

Choose the right answer.

LEVEL 3

1 tome
    a a traditional story
    b a sort of elf
    c a heavy book

2 dromedary
    a a Greek coin
    b the study of old civilisations
    c an animal with a hump

3 salamander
    a an animal like a newt
    b a special way of dancing
    c a dishonest person

4 Namibia
    a a country in Africa
    b a brightly coloured cloth
    c a skin disease

5 retina
    a sap from a pine tree
    b a red wine
    c part of the eye

6 magenta
    a a purple colour
    b an award given for bravery
    c a type of horse

7 canyon
    a a large gun that fires cannon balls
    b a deep valley between cliffs
    c a priest

8 yam
    a a small coin in Egypt
    b a type of root vegetable
    c a cow that can live in hot climates

9 rodeo
    a a small, rat-like animal
    b a road that crosses a river
    c a competition for cowboys

Activity 2: What do they do?

Teaching notes

Pupils may have heard of many of these words, and it is often easy to guess what they mean. Most of the words have a fairly closed meaning, for example a *dentist* or a *trombonist* can really mean only one thing. Talking about these words and their meanings helps to develop your pupils' vocabulary and awareness of the range of human pursuits, which can be especially valuable for pupils who lack stimulating language environments at home.

Some words can generate interesting classroom discussion and debate. For example, how do you define an *artist*? Is it someone who creates anything beautiful? Could a gardener or someone who knits be an artist? Can anyone be a *scientist* just by looking and thinking? Is someone who uses a parachute to escape from a burning plane a parachutist or not? Is someone who rides a tricycle or a monocycle still a cyclist?

Level 1

1 Looks after people's teeth.
2 Rides a cycle.
3 Creates something beautiful.
4 Investigates and experiments to find out new things.
5 Plays the piano.
6 Drives a car.
7 Visits places that are interesting.
8 Draws cartoons.
9 Jumps from a plane using a parachute.

Level 2

1 Understands chemicals and can use them, e.g. for medicines.
2 Plays a guitar.
3 Travels in a hot-air balloon.
4 Plays the violin.
5 Is a type of scientist who studies plants or animals.
6 Plays the trombone.
7 Types, usually in an office.
8 Is a solo performer, e.g. a singer or musician.
9 Sells flowers, or makes floral arrangements.

Level 3

1 Sings, often with a band.
2 Looks after people's fingernails and toenails.
3 Hypnotises people.
4 Operates a machine, e.g. a sewing machine.
5 Treats people with illnesses or problems.
6 Is a type of scientist who studies plants.
7 Looks on the bright side; does not expect bad things to happen.
8 Is a type of criminal who deliberately sets property on fire.
9 Believes in peace and will not fight or go to war.

Activity 2

What do they do?

LEVEL 1

What do these people do?

1 dentist

2 cyclist

3 artist

4 scientist

5 pianist

6 motorist

7 tourist

8 cartoonist

9 parachutist

From: *Spotlight on Your Inclusive Classroom*, Routledge © Glynis Hannell 2009

Activity 2

What do they do?

LEVEL 2

What do these people do?

1 chemist

2 guitarist

3 balloonist

4 violinist

5 biologist

6 trombonist

7 typist

8 soloist

9 florist

Activity 2

What do they do?

LEVEL 3

What do these people do?

1 vocalist

2 manicurist

3 hypnotist

4 machinist

5 therapist

6 botanist

7 optimist

8 arsonist

9 pacifist

Activity 3: Animal babies and groups

Teaching notes

Learning about *Animal babies and groups* helps to increase vocabulary and enrich your pupils' language skills. Children can, of course, 'make do' with phrases such as *a baby cow*, *a little pig* or *a lot of elephants*. But their language skills are significantly improved if they can understand and use words such as *calf*, *piglet* or *herd*.

There are alternatives to some of these items, for example a group of ants can be called *an army of ants* as well as *a colony of ants*. Pupils may enjoy researching suggested alternatives to see if they are acceptable.

Level 1

1 kitten

2 puppy

3 chick

4 piglet

5 flock

6 herd

7 litter

8 pack

Level 2

1 cub

2 calf

3 foal

4 joey

5 pride

6 pod

7 swarm

8 troop

Level 3

1 tadpole

2 signet

3 fledgling or chick

4 kid

5 colony

6 herd

7 school

8 gaggle

Activity 3

Animal babies and groups

LEVEL 1

Complete the sentences.

1 A baby cat is called a _____ .

2 A baby dog is called a _____ .

3 A baby chicken is called a _____ .

4 A baby pig is called a _____ .

5 A group of birds is called a _____ of birds.

6 A group of cows is called a _____ of cows.

7 A group of kittens is called a _____ of kittens.

8 A group of wolves is called a _____ of wolves.

Activity 3

Animal babies and groups

LEVEL 2

Complete the sentences.

1 A baby lion is called a _____.

2 A baby cow is called a _____.

3 A baby horse is called a _____.

4 A baby kangaroo is called a _____.

5 A group of lions is called a _____ of lions.

6 A group of dolphins is called a _____ of dolphins.

7 A group of bees is called a _____ of bees.

8 A group of monkeys is called a _____ of monkeys.

From: *Spotlight on Your Inclusive Classroom*, Routledge © Glynis Hannell 2009

Activity 3

Animal babies and groups

LEVEL 3

Complete the sentences.

1 A baby frog is called a _____.

2 A baby swan is called a _____.

3 A baby bird is called a _____.

4 A baby goat is called a _____.

5 A group of ants is called a _____ of ants.

6 A group of elephants is called a _____ of elephants.

7 A group of fish is called a _____ of fish.

8 A group of geese is called a _____ of geese.

From: *Spotlight on Your Inclusive Classroom*, Routledge © Glynis Hannell 2009

Activity 4: Synonyms

Teaching notes

Learning about *Synonyms* (words that mean the same) can enhance pupils' vocabularies. The process of finding synonyms challenges them to think very carefully about what words mean. For example, does *nice* really mean the same as *lovely*? Could *huge* mean the same as *big*, or does it match *enormous* better?

Encourage the pupils to think of as many alternatives as possible. This activity can stimulate good discussion about words and their meanings. This can draw the pupils' attention to the subtle distinctions between one word and another and help those with less well-developed language skills to understand how words can be defined, compared and refined. Enhanced skills in the use of synonyms will also help all your pupils to improve their written expression.

Level 1

1 store, supermarket

2 beautiful, pretty

3 speak

4 shout

5 chair

6 quick

7 large

8 ill, unwell

9 more

Level 2

1 glasses, eyeglasses

2 handle

3 stone

4 end

5 keep

6 tug

7 sleep

8 like

9 broad

Level 3

1 quiet

2 pill

3 tired

4 careful

5 lazy

6 sure

7 strength

8 pail

9 remain

Activity 4

Synonyms

LEVEL 1

Find another word that means the same.

1 shop _____

2 lovely _____

3 talk _____

4 yell _____

5 seat _____

6 fast _____

7 big _____

8 sick _____

9 extra _____

From: *Spotlight on Your Inclusive Classroom*, Routledge © Glynis Hannell 2009

Activity 4

Synonyms

LEVEL 2

Find another word that means the same.

1   spectacles   _____

2   knob   _____

3   pebble   _____

4   finish   _____

5   save   _____

6   pull   _____

7   snooze   _____

8   enjoy   _____

9   wide   _____

Activity 4

Synonyms

LEVEL 3

Find another word that means the same.

1 silent _____

2 tablet _____

3 weary _____

4 cautious _____

5 idle _____

6 certain _____

7 power _____

8 bucket _____

9 stay _____

From: *Spotlight on Your Inclusive Classroom*, Routledge © Glynis Hannell 2009

Activity 5: Same and different

Teaching notes

Same and different helps to develop logical thinking. Your pupils will need to think flexibly. First, they need to think of the connection between two words and then twist their thinking around the other way to think of differences. This is a good cognitive activity and helps to develop flexible thinking.

Encourage discussion. There can be several ways of looking at these similarities and differences. The classroom discussion itself can help to build the pupils' language skills.

Level 1

	Same	*Different*
1	fly	animal/machine
2	clothing	head/foot
3	transport	land/water
4	sweet spreads bees/humans	made by
5	words	see words/ make words
6	seasoning for food	hot taste/salty taste
7	cold, white	cream, manmade/ water, natural
8	see-through	solid/liquid
9	physical need, sensation	food/liquid

Level 2

	Same	*Different*
1	male	older/younger
2	seasons of the year	cold/warm
3	drinks	animal/fruit
4	cleansing	manufactured, lathers/natural, does not lather
5	milk products	natural milk/ processed milk
6	animals live there	caged/roaming free
7	transport with pedals	two wheels/ three wheels
8	primates	small/large
9	movement in water	on the surface/ under water

Level 3

	Same	*Different*
1	sharp, sewing	head, no eye/ no head, eye
2	bodies of salt water	larger/smaller
3	natural disasters	strong winds/ strong Earth movements
4	cattle	male/female
5	natural fibres	animal origin/ plant origin
6	force out of shape	turn in opposite directions/fold in one direction
7	ways of seeing something	see-through/cannot be seen at all
8	secret messages	secret word/ substitute symbols are used
9	natural surface of the Earth	fertile/infertile

Activity 5

Same and different

LEVEL 1

How are these pairs of words the same? How are these pairs of words different?

1   bird and plane   _____

_____

2   hat and shoe   _____

_____

3   car and boat   _____

_____

4   honey and jam   _____

_____

5   reading and writing   _____

_____

6   pepper and salt   _____

_____

7   ice cream and snow   _____

_____

8   glass and water   _____

_____

9   hungry and thirsty   _____

_____

Activity 5

Same and different

LEVEL 2

How are these pairs of words the same? How are these pairs of words different?

1 man and a boy _____
_____

2 winter and summer _____
_____

3 milk and orange juice _____
_____

4 soap and water _____
_____

5 milk and yoghurt _____
_____

6 zoo and wildlife park _____
_____

7 bicycle and tricycle _____
_____

8 monkey and gorilla _____
_____

9 swim and dive _____
_____

Activity 5

Same and different

LEVEL 3

How are these pairs of words the same? How are these pairs of words different?

1 pins and needles _____
_____

2 oceans and seas _____
_____

3 hurricane and earthquake _____
_____

4 bull and cow _____
_____

5 wool and cotton _____
_____

6 twist and bend _____
_____

7 transparent and invisible _____
_____

8 password and code _____
_____

9 soil and sand _____
_____

From: *Spotlight on Your Inclusive Classroom*, Routledge © Glynis Hannell 2009

Activity 6: Parts

Teaching notes

Parts is another vocabulary developer that will particularly help pupils with limited language skills. It also encourages the pupils to visualise the objects and analyse the parts, or components, of each. This develops logical systematic thinking, as the pupils discover that random naming works less well than careful, methodical naming! Some items only have a few components, while others have an almost infinite number! Encourage pupils to research items when they run out of ideas, for example an egg has more parts than you might think!

Level 1

1   sole, upper, heel, eyelets, inner sole, tongue . . .

2   eyebrows, eyes, nose, nostrils, mouth, chin, cheeks . . .

3   wheels, kickboard, handlebars, foot brake, axle . . .

4   walls, roof, floor, stairs, windows, chimney . . .

5   tail, fins, scales, eyes, mouth, heart . . .

6   cover, spine, pages, pictures, words, title . . .

7   wheels, engine, chassis, seats, steering wheel . . .

8   trunk, branches, twigs, leaves, buds, flowers, fruit, roots, bark . . .

9   frame, mattress, legs, sheet, pillow . . .

Level 2

1   sleeves, collar, front, back, buttons, buttonholes . . .

2   thigh, knee, calf, ankle, skin, hair, muscles . . .

3   wheels, spokes, brakes, seat, handlebars . . .

4   walls, roof, floor, windows, entry, classroom, hall . . .

5   head, body, wings, feet, feathers, eyes, tail . . .

6   shell, yolk, albumen, membrane . . .

7   stem, petals, stamens, sepal . . .

8   engine, carriages, wheels, guards van, seat, luggage racks . . .

9   wooden case, white keys, black keys, strings, pedals . . .

Level 3

1   legs, waistband, zip, pockets, seams . . .

2   iris, pupil, retina, lens . . .

3   hull, mast, keel, sails, ropes, rudder, tiller . . .

4   wings, head, thorax, abdomen, legs . . .

5   fuselage, wings, cockpit, tail, undercarriage . . .

6   lens, case, zoom control, flash, timer, memory card . . .

7   body, legs, head, tail, ears, fur, claws . . .

8   upper arm, forearm, elbow, wrist, humerus, radius, ulna

9   case, keyboard, space bar, USB ports, mouse, microchip . . .

Activity 6

Parts

LEVEL 1

How many parts can you name?

1 shoe _____

2 face _____

3 scooter _____

4 house _____

5 fish _____

6 book _____

7 car _____

8 tree _____

9 bed _____

Activity 6

Parts

LEVEL 2

How many parts can you name?

1 shirt _____

2 leg _____

3 bicycle _____

4 school building _____

5 bird _____

6 egg _____

7 flower _____

8 train _____

9 piano _____

Activity 6

Parts

LEVEL 3

How many parts can you name?

1 jeans _____

2 eye _____

3 sailing
boat _____

4 butterfly _____

5 aeroplane _____

6 camera _____

7 dog _____

8 arm _____

9 computer _____

From: *Spotlight on Your Inclusive Classroom*, Routledge © Glynis Hannell 2009

Activity 7: Idioms

Teaching notes

Being able to understand and use *Idioms* is part and parcel of being able to communicate effectively. This activity will help you to accelerate your pupils' understanding of idiomatic speech. The activity may also excite the pupils' curiosity and get them asking what other idioms mean. Your class might enjoy making their own collection of idioms that they hear.

Level 1

1 Jane's book looked [a mess].

2 [Slow down], Becky!

3 Sam [was in a bad mood].

4 You [said exactly the right thing].

5 It was raining [very heavily] when we walked home.

6 Paul was feeling [unwell].

7 Philip told Jess to [think cleverly].

8 You would eat cake [for a long time].

9 It snows [very rarely].

Level 2

1 [There are bad things coming] for her.

2 David scored [three in a row].

3 Belle's plans [did not turn out as well as expected].

4 All their money has [disappeared].

5 Tim [walked] home.

6 The baby was [Grandma's favourite].

7 Mum said she [would not have anything to do with] the party.

8 Len [hid the truth from Dad].

9 They [had a very narrow escape].

Level 3

1 I thought Prue was [trying too hard to improve something already perfect].

2 Stan always seemed to [be resentful and angry].

3 The news came [very suddenly and unexpectedly].

4 Peg and Fred will [show you what to do].

5 Saying you don't like her dress is just [mean because you are jealous].

6 Helen asked Ted, 'When shall we [get married]?'

7 The teacher [pretended not to notice] when Josh came in late.

8 When I told you Harry was handsome it was [insincere, as he is not handsome at all].

9 Ned said, 'I have a little [money that has been saved up] that we could use.'

Activity 7

Idioms

LEVEL 1

What do these sentences mean?

1 Jane's book looked like a dog's dinner.

2 Hold your horses, Becky!

3 Sam got out on the wrong side of the bed.

4 You hit the nail on the head.

5 It was raining cats and dogs when we walked home.

6 Paul was feeling under the weather.

7 Philip told Jess to use her loaf.

8 You would eat cake until the cows came home.

9 It snows once in a blue moon.

From: *Spotlight on Your Inclusive Classroom*, Routledge © Glynis Hannell 2009

Activity 7

Idioms

LEVEL 2

What do these sentences mean?

1 The writing is on the wall for her.

2 David scored a hat-trick.

3 Belle's plans went pear-shaped.

4 All their money has gone west.

5 Tim used Shanks's pony to get home.

6 The baby was the apple of Grandma's eye.

7 Mum said she had washed her hands of the party.

8 Len pulled the wool over Dad's eyes.

9 They escaped by the skin of their teeth.

Activity 7

Idioms

LEVEL 3

What do these sentences mean?

1   I thought Prue was gilding the lily.

2   Stan always seemed to have a chip on his shoulder.

3   The news came like a bolt from the blue.

4   Peg and Fred will show you the ropes.

5   Saying you don't like her dress is just sour grapes.

6   Helen asked Ted, 'When shall we tie the knot?'

7   The teacher turned a blind eye when Josh came in late.

8   When I told you Harry was handsome it was tongue in cheek.

9   Ned said, 'I have a little nest egg that we could use.'

From: *Spotlight on Your Inclusive Classroom*, Routledge © Glynis Hannell 2009

Activity 8: Proverbs

Teaching notes

As well as introducing pupils to an important aspect of language, *Proverbs* also provides additional benefits. Many younger or less able pupils are very literal in their thinking. Talking about proverbs helps to foster pupils' abstract reasoning and general cognitive development. In addition, the practical and moral principles behind these sayings give teachers an opportunity to build their pupils' social insight, which in turn underpins healthy personal development.

This activity is intended as a classroom discussion activity, where pupils and teachers look at each proverb and discuss what it means. It is particularly helpful if teachers can link the proverbs into the real-life, practical experiences of their pupils.

The following are the proverbs used in this activity.

Level 1

1 Slow but sure wins the race.

2 Practice makes perfect.

3 The early bird catches the worm.

4 Look before you leap.

5 You can't have your cake and eat it.

6 It's no use crying over spilt milk.

7 Many hands make light work.

8 Learn to walk before you can run.

9 Two heads are better than one.

Level 2

1 All work and no play make Jack a dull boy.

2 Birds of a feather flock together.

3 Make hay while the sun shines.

4 The proof of the pudding is in the eating.

5 One good turn deserves another.

6 It's too late to lock the stable door when the horse has bolted.

7 There no smoke without fire.

8 Don't make a mountain out of a molehill.

9 Never look a gift horse in the mouth.

Level 3

1 Don't put all your eggs in one basket.

2 Waste not, want not.

3 Jack of all trades and master of none.

4 A rolling stone gathers no moss.

5 Variety is the spice of life.

6 A bad workman blames his tools.

7 Absence makes the heart grow fonder.

8 Empty vessels make the most noise.

9 Don't wash your dirty linen in public.

Activity 8

Proverbs

LEVEL 1

What do these proverbs mean?

1   Slow but sure wins the race.

2   Practice makes perfect.

3   The early bird catches the worm.

4   Look before you leap.

5   You can't have your cake and eat it.

6   It's no use crying over spilt milk.

7   Many hands make light work.

8   Learn to walk before you can run.

9   Two heads are better than one.

   From: *Spotlight on Your Inclusive Classroom*, Routledge © Glynis Hannell 2009

Activity 8

Proverbs

LEVEL 2

What do these proverbs mean?

1 All work and no play make Jack a dull boy.

2 Birds of a feather flock together.

3 Make hay while the sun shines.

4 The proof of the pudding is in the eating.

5 One good turn deserves another.

6 It's too late to lock the stable door when the horse has bolted.

7 There no smoke without fire.

8 Don't make a mountain out of a molehill.

9 Never look a gift horse in the mouth.

Activity 8

Proverbs

LEVEL 3

What do these proverbs mean?

1 Don't put all your eggs in one basket.

2 Waste not, want not.

3 Jack of all trades and master of none.

4 A rolling stone gathers no moss.

5 Variety is the spice of life.

6 A bad workman blames his tools.

7 Absence makes the heart grow fonder.

8 Empty vessels make the most noise.

9 Don't wash your dirty linen in public.

CHAPTER 3

Mathematics

A sense of number

Before pupils can successfully work mathematically they need to have a *sense of number*. This does not entail performing detailed calculations, but rather relates to the pupil's ability to judge what might be reasonable, or unreasonable, in a given situation. For example, numerate pupils will understand that, in terms of order of magnitude, 1,000 is much, much larger than 12, even if they cannot give a mathematical value for the difference between these two numbers.

Pupils with a sense of number will be able to judge what would be a likely number to a given question, and reject an answer that intuitively seems wrong. This is an important foundation for accurate mathematical work. Errors do occur in computation, or in the use of a calculator, and pupils who lack good number sense will be disadvantaged because they will not readily pick up any errors that they make.

A sense of number also depends on understanding imprecise information such as *nearly all*, *except a few*, *more than usual*, *less than half* and so on, and being able to relate it to a probable answer.

Estimating (Activity 9) and *True or false?* (Activity 14) give pupils practice at estimating rather than calculating.

Of course, accurate computation and familiarity with the way in which numbers 'work' are also important parts of mathematical ability. *Make this number* (Activity 11), *What number am I?* (Activity 12) and *At the zoo* (Activity 13) give your pupils practice in exact calculations.

In this brief chapter, your pupils will be able to sample various mathematical activities that will promote their understanding of our number system and calendar, strengthen their ability to estimate, and give practice in performing specific calculations with whole numbers and fractions.

Activity 9: Estimating

Teaching notes

Estimating encourages your pupils to *estimate* rather than *calculate*. Some pupils are very unsure of themselves in doing this, and may need to be encouraged to simply have a try and see if they can apply general logic and numerical commonsense instead of trying to work out the correct answer. Note that, in some questions, the correct answer is not given, only a close approximation, so that pupils will be forced to make a judgement on the nearest, rather than the exact answer.

Note: The questions demand quite good reading skills, so teachers should work through the items orally with those pupils whose reading is limited.

Level 1

1 8

2 4

3 70

4 13

5 2

6 56

7 28

8 26

9 15

Level 2

1 £1

2 34

3 £25

4 7

5 37

6 15 weeks

7 23

8 40

9 15

Level 3

1 3,000

2 4.45

3 Just over 30 minutes

4 10 for £5

5 41

6 Between £10 and £11

7 26

8 95

9 150

Activity 9

Estimating

LEVEL 1

Choose the most likely answer to these questions.

1 Mum cut up the birthday cake so everyone in the family could have
a piece. About how many pieces of cake were there?

        2   8   100

2 About how many pips are there in an apple?

        4   24   50

3 How many people can fit on a double decker bus?

        5   70   300

4 The baby has about 6 clean nappies every day. How many nappies
did the baby need for 2 days?

      13   5   8

5 A car can carry 4 or 5 people. How many cars would you need for
10 people?

      6   2   1

6 The pupils in the class took off their shoes. About how many shoes
were there altogether?

     56   18   87

7 There are about 10 pencils in each jar. How many pencils in 3 jars?

      5   60   28

8 There were 28 children in the class and nearly all of them went to
the zoo. How many children went to the zoo?

      3   12   26

9 How many children in your class might have a pet at home?

     15   60   2

Activity 9

Estimating

Choose the most likely answer to these questions.

LEVEL 2

1   A large ice cream costs £2. How much will a small ice cream cost?

   £1   £10   5p

2   Sam is 7 years old. How old is his mother?

   12   86   34

3   T-shirts cost around £8 each. About how much will you pay for 3 T-shirts?

   £25   £100   £18

4   Usually there are about 3 or 4 dogs in the park, but today there were a few more than usual. How many dogs were there?

   4   7   28

5   Monkeys have about 3 bananas each for breakfast. How many bananas will the zookeeper need to feed 12 monkeys?

   37   21   80

6   The battery in Tim's remote control car lasts for about 4 weeks. If he buys a pack of 4 batteries, how many weeks will they last?

   44   15   1

7   Ducks have about 6 ducklings each. There are 4 ducks on my pond, so about how many ducklings will there be?

   23   12   60

8   Jack had 12 jelly babies, Paula had 20 jelly babies and Ross had 5 jelly babies. About how many did they have altogether?

   40   30   50

9   The teacher had 32 coloured pencils to share between 2 groups. About how many coloured pencils did each group get?

   15   30   6

Activity 9

Estimating

Choose the most likely answer to these questions.   **LEVEL 3**

1 A box of rice bubbles will be enough for 6 people to have one bowl each. Each bowl contains about 450 rice bubbles. How many rice bubbles in the box?

        100   50,000   3,000

2 George was supposed to be home by 4.30 in the afternoon, but he was a little bit late. About what time did he get home?

       4.45   4.20   5.30

3 The train could travel at 100 miles an hour. How long did it take to travel 60 miles?

  About 10 minutes   Just over 30 minutes Just under 30 minutes

4 What is the best deal for buying blank CDs?

     5 for £2   10 for £5   50 for £75

5 Most houses in my street have 2 TV sets, but some houses have 3 TV sets. There are 20 houses in the street. About how many TV sets are there altogether?

       41   38   75

6 Stamps cost 20p each. I had about 52 invitations to send out, so how much did I spend on stamps?

  Less than £5   Between £10 and £11   Over £11

7 The Tigers team usually scored 2 or 3 goals each match. They played 10 matches. How many goals did they score altogether?

       18   32   26

8 There are 15 steps up to the art room. If the teacher goes up the steps 6 or 7 times, about how many steps has she climbed?

       95   110   65

9 Each swimming squad has about 24 children. There were 6 squads at a swimming carnival, so how many children took part?

      150   240   64

Activity 10: Calendar

Teaching notes

Calendar is based on the Gregorian calendar, as this is the international standard. However, teachers will be aware that other calendars, such as the Hebrew, Islamic, Indian, Chinese, Hindu or Buddhist calendars, may also be in use in pupils' homes. Generally, these will be used alongside the Gregorian calendar for cultural and religious purposes. It is appropriate for teachers to remind their pupils that the calendar we use is, in fact, one of many.

Level 1

1 morning
2 7
3 spring, summer, autumn, winter
4 Thursday
5 Monday
6 spring
7 January
8 12
9 sunrise

Level 2

1 14 days
2 October

3 February
4 December
5 February
6 1 January
7 100 years
8 12 pm
9 September, April, June, November

Level 3

1 once every 29 or 30 days
2 June
3 31 December
4 once a year
5 10 years
6 exactly one year after
7 31 December 1799
8 when the sun is directly over the equator, on around 20 March and 22 September each year
9 *ante meridiem*, before midday; *post meridiem*, after midday

Activity 10

Calendar

LEVEL 1

Answer these questions.

1 Which comes first each day, morning or afternoon?

2 How many days are there in a week?

3 What are the seasons of the year?

4 Which day comes after Wednesday?

5 Which day comes before Tuesday?

6 Which season comes after winter?

7 What is the first month of the year?

8 How many months are there in the year?

9 Which comes first, sunset or sunrise?

Activity 10

Calendar

LEVEL 2

Answer these questions.

1   How long is a fortnight?

2   What is the tenth month of the year?

3   Which month has an extra day once every four years?

4   What is the last month of the year?

5   What is the shortest month of the year?

6   What date is it on New Year's Day?

7   What is a century?

8   What is the time at midnight?

9   Which months of the year have thirty days in them?

From: *Spotlight on Your Inclusive Classroom*, Routledge © Glynis Hannell 2009

Activity 10

Calendar

LEVEL 3

Answer these questions.

1   How often is there a full moon?

2   Which month has the longest day?

3   What is the date of the last day of the year?

4   How often does an annual event happen?

5   What is a decade?

6   What is an anniversary?

7   On what date did the eighteenth century end?

8   What is the equinox?

9   What do am and pm mean?

Activity 11: Make this number

Teaching notes

In *Make this number* pupils are asked to reach a target number by manipulating the set of numbers provided. The numbers can be added, subtracted, multiplied or divided to arrive at the target number.

Here are some samples of the activity. Use the opportunity to talk to the pupils about the various ways in which the target number can be arrived at.

Level 1

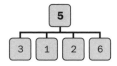

$3 + 2 = 5$

$6 - 1 = 5$

$[6 + 2] - 3 = 5$

$[6 - 2] + 1 = 5$

$5 - 3 = 2$

$6 \div 3 = 2$

$6 - 3 - 1 = 2$

Level 2

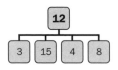

$15 - 3 = 12$

$4 + 8 = 12$

$3 \times 4 = 12$

$10 + 2 + 1 = 13$

$15 - 2 - 1 = 13$

Level 3

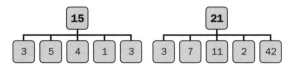

$3 \times 5 = 15$

$[3 \times 4] + 3 = 15$

$[5 \times 4] - [3 + 3]$
$\quad + 1 = 15$

$3 \times 7 = 21$

$42 \div 2 = 21$

$3 + 7 + 11 = 21$

Activity 11

Make this number

LEVEL 1

See the number in the box above the line? This is the *target* number. Use the numbers in the boxes below the line to make the target number. You can add, subtract, multiply or divide these numbers.

1

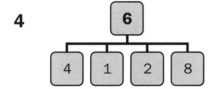

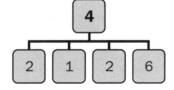

2

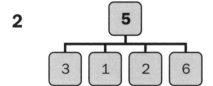

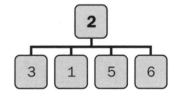

3

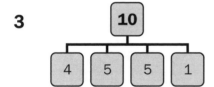

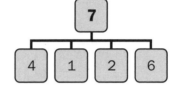

4

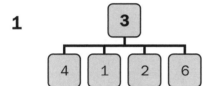

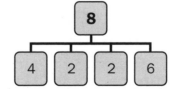

Activity 11

Make this number

LEVEL 2

See the number in the box above the line? This is the *target* number. Use the numbers in the boxes below the line to make the target number. You can add, subtract, multiply or divide these numbers.

1

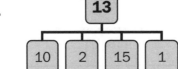

13 | 10 | 2 | 15 | 1

12 | 3 | 15 | 4 | 8

2

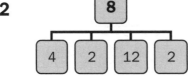

8 | 4 | 2 | 12 | 2

9 | 3 | 12 | 6 | 4

3

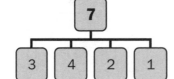
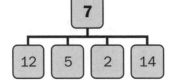

7 | 12 | 5 | 2 | 14

20 | 15 | 5 | 30 | 4

4

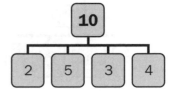
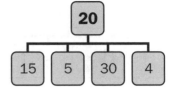
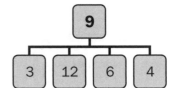
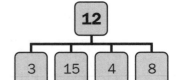

7 | 3 | 4 | 2 | 1

10 | 2 | 5 | 3 | 4

Activity 11

Make this number

LEVEL 3

See the number in the box above the line? This is the *target* number. Use the numbers in the boxes below the line to make the target number. You can add, subtract, multiply or divide these numbers.

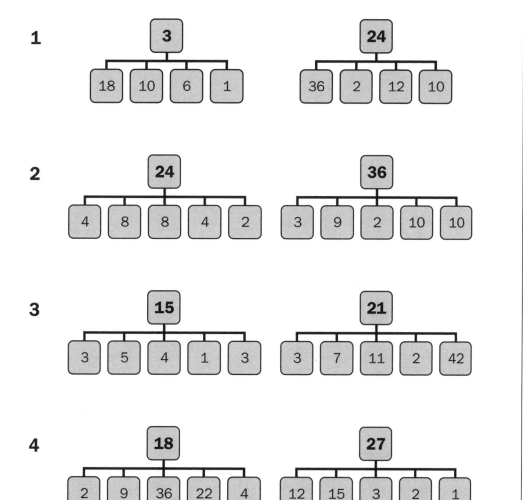

1

| 3 |
| 18 | 10 | 6 | 1 |

| 24 |
| 36 | 2 | 12 | 10 |

2

| 24 |
| 4 | 8 | 8 | 4 | 2 |

| 36 |
| 3 | 9 | 2 | 10 | 10 |

3

| 15 |
| 3 | 5 | 4 | 1 | 3 |

| 21 |
| 3 | 7 | 11 | 2 | 42 |

4

| 18 |
| 2 | 9 | 36 | 22 | 4 |

| 27 |
| 12 | 15 | 3 | 2 | 1 |

Activity 12: What number am I?

Teaching notes

The ability to think about numbers and their relationship to each other is the foundation of mental computation, estimating and 'number sense'. *What number am I?* encourages pupils to visualise a number line and place numbers in position, work with the composition and decomposition of numbers, work with 'doubles' and 'halves' and perform mental arithmetic tasks that require two or more stages of thinking. These questions help to promote your pupils' mathematical agility, which is so important in real-life situations.

Level 1

1 2
2 7
3 6
4 9
5 5
6 10
7 9
8 10
9 12

Level 2

1 10
2 5
3 9
4 14
5 14
6 6
7 16
8 9
9 10

Level 3

1 10
2 18
3 25
4 26
5 10
6 12
7 20
8 14
9 15

Activity 12

What number am I?

LEVEL 1

What number am I?

1 I am smaller than 3 but bigger than 1. _____

2 I am between 6 and 8. _____

3 I am twice as big as 3. _____

4 I am one smaller than 10. _____

5 I am as big as 3 and 2 added together. _____

6 If I lose 3 I will only be 7. _____

7 I am an odd number bigger than 8 and smaller than 11. _____

8 I need 2 more to make me 12. _____

9 If you cut me in half I will be 6. _____

Activity 12

What number am I?

LEVEL 2

What number am I?

1 I am twice as big as 5. _____

2 I need 3 more to make me 8. _____

3 I am just as big as 5 added to 3 added to 1.
_____

4 I am an even number between 12 and 16.
_____

5 If I lose 6 I will only be 8. _____

6 If I get 6 more I will be 12. _____

7 If you cut me in half I will be 8. _____

8 If I lose 4 and add 2 I will be 7. _____

9 I am double 4 added to 2. _____

Activity 12

What number am I?

LEVEL 3

What number am I?

1 I am 20 cut in half. _____

2 I can be divided by 3 and I am between 17 and 20. _____

3 I am double 12 with 1 added on. _____

4 If I lose 10 I will only be 16. _____

5 If I double and then double again I will be 40.
_____

6 I can be divided by 4 and also divided by 3. I am between 10 and 20. _____

7 I am 4 times larger than 5. _____

8 I am 1 less than half of 30. _____

9 I am half of 8 added to half of 22. _____

Activity 13: At the zoo

Teaching notes

Here is something to really challenge your pupils' mathematical thinking. *At the zoo* provides excellent opportunities for teachers to work with a group, discussing strategies, calculating solutions and exploring whole numbers and fractions together. This is designed as a teacher-led exercise. Only the most able pupils would be expected to complete the activity independently.

Paper and pencil will be essential as many pupils will need to use diagrams or tally marks. Some will need to use concrete counting materials, such as paper bananas, cut into fractions to help with the calculation. Although challenging, this activity can really help to make fractions 'come alive' for your pupils. Following are the banana allowances (not all levels use all the allowances), and then the answers.

marmoset	$\frac{1}{4}$ banana a day
capuchin monkey	$\frac{3}{4}$ banana a day
spider monkey	$\frac{1}{2}$ banana a day
howler monkey	1 banana a day
orang-utan	2 bananas a day

Level 1

1   5

2   4

3   1

4   2

5   5

6   12

7   $10\frac{1}{2}$

8   15

9   14

Level 2

1   $9\frac{1}{4}$

2   13

3   $1\frac{1}{2}$

4   $4\frac{3}{4}$

5   21

6   1

7   $\frac{3}{4}$

8   7

9   $9\frac{3}{4}$

Level 3

1   1

2   $1\frac{1}{2}$

3   3

4   $12\frac{3}{4}$

5   7

6   18

7   $15\frac{1}{2}$

8   15

9   12

Activity 13

At the zoo

LEVEL 1

Cathy, the zookeeper, has to feed the animals bananas. Here is her list of what they eat:

spider monkey $\frac{1}{2}$ banana a day
howler monkey 1 banana a day
orang-utan 2 bananas a day.

How many bananas does Cathy need to feed these animals?

1 5 howler monkeys for 1 day

2 2 orang-utans for 1 day

3 2 spider monkeys for 1 day

4 2 spider monkeys and 1 howler monkey for 1 day

5 2 spider monkeys, 2 howler monkeys and
1 orang-utan for 1 day

6 6 howler monkeys and 3 orang-utans for 1 day

7 3 spider monkeys, 3 howler monkeys and
3 orang-utans for 1 day

8 1 spider monkey, 5 howler monkeys and
1 orang-utan for 2 days

9 2 spider monkeys, 2 howler monkeys and
2 orang-utans for 2 days

From: *Spotlight on Your Inclusive Classroom*, Routledge © Glynis Hannell 2009

Activity 13

At the zoo

LEVEL 2

Cathy, the zookeeper, has to feed the animals bananas. Here is her list of what they eat:

marmoset	$\frac{1}{4}$ banana a day
spider monkey	$\frac{1}{2}$ banana a day
howler monkey	1 banana a day
orang-utan	2 bananas a day.

How many bananas does Cathy need to feed these animals?

1 1 marmoset, 5 howler monkeys and 2 orang-utans for 1 day

2 2 spider monkeys and 6 orang-utans for 1 day

3 2 marmosets and 2 spider monkeys for 1 day

4 3 marmosets, 4 spider monkeys and 1 orang-utan for 1 day

5 4 marmosets, 10 howler monkeys and 5 orang-utans for 1 day

6 2 marmosets and 1 spider monkey for 1 day

7 1 marmoset and 1 spider monkey for 1 day

8 1 spider monkey, 1 howler monkey and 1 orang-utan for 2 days

9 1 marmoset, 1 howler monkey and 1 orang-utan for 3 days

Activity 13

At the zoo

LEVEL 3

Cathy, the zookeeper, has to feed the animals bananas. Here is her list of what they eat:

marmoset	$\frac{1}{4}$ banana a day
capuchin monkey	$\frac{3}{4}$ banana a day
spider monkey	$\frac{1}{2}$ banana a day
howler monkey	1 banana a day
orang-utan	2 bananas a day.

How many bananas does Cathy need to feed these animals?

1   1 marmoset and 1 capuchin monkey for 1 day

2   1 marmoset, 1 capuchin monkey and 1 spider monkey for 1 day

3   2 capuchin monkeys and 3 spider monkeys for 1 day

4   1 marmoset, 1 spider monkey and 6 orang-utans for 1 day

5   4 marmosets, 4 spider monkeys and 4 howler monkeys for 1 day

6   8 marmosets and 8 orang-utans for 1 day

7   1 marmoset, 1 spider monkey and 7 howler monkeys for 2 days

8   1 capuchin monkey and 6 spider monkeys for 4 days

9   6 marmosets, 6 capuchin monkeys and 6 howler monkeys for 1 day

Activity 14: True or false?

Teaching notes

True or false? contains mixed items that exercise your pupils' mathematical thinking and estimating skills. This is a good group or class activity. Thinking strategies as well as actual calculation can be modelled so that all pupils learn how to think about mathematical questions.

Level 1

1   false

2   true

3   true

4   false

5   true

6   false

7   true

8   false

9   false

Level 2

1   true

2   true

3   false

4   false

5   true

6   true

7   true

8   true

9   false

Level 3

1   true

2   false

3   true

4   true

5   false

6   false

7   true

8   false

9   true

Activity 14

True or false?

LEVEL 1

Are these true or false?

1 A small bag of jelly beans
costs about £20.   _____

2 You can buy milk in
1 litre cartons.   _____

3 With 50p you could buy
2 chocolate frogs at 20p each.   _____

4 Ava, Gina and Hannah have £2 each.
They have £12 altogether.   _____

5 Double 6 is 12.   _____

6 16 is bigger than 18.   _____

7 3 + 3 + 3 + 3 = 12.   _____

8 There are 20 steps, then another
15 steps. There are 50 steps.   _____

9 You could eat 5 kilos of apples
at once.   _____

Activity 14

True or false?

LEVEL 2

Are these true or false?

1   An adult man could be
2 metres tall.   _____

2   120 is bigger than 119.   _____

3   You should drink about 20 litres
of water a day.   _____

4   If you buy a 75p comb with a
£1 coin you get 20p change.   _____

5   Jack is 1.32 metres tall and
Kyle is 1.70. Kyle is the tallest. _____

6   35 is half of 70.   _____

7   Chewy bars cost 75p each. A bag
of 10 for £7 is a good deal.   _____

8   40 + 30 + 30 + 30 = 130.   _____

9   25 people fit in one bus. You need
6 buses for 100 people.   _____

    From: *Spotlight on Your Inclusive Classroom*, Routledge © Glynis Hannell 2009

Activity 14

True or false?

LEVEL 3

Are these true or false?

1 An apple weighs about
150 grams.   _____

2 A bedroom is usually 30 metres long
and 20 metres wide.   _____

3 65 is exactly halfway between
50 and 80.   _____

4 A small bottle of soft drink contains
about 375 millilitres of liquid.   _____

5 If you had £20 you could buy
6 pens at £3.95 each.   _____

6 Half of 144 is 74.   _____

7 250 + 250 + 250 + 250 = 1000.   _____

8 T-shirts cost £8 each.
3 for £28 is a good deal.   _____

9 If the groceries cost £97.63 you
will get £2.37 change from £100.   _____

CHAPTER 4

The world around us

General knowledge

We live in an amazing world, where there are so many fascinating things to discover and understand. It is fun when pupils' curiosity is aroused and they begin to think about the world around them, ask questions, find answers and begin to fit the jigsaw of information together.

One of the most alienating experiences for any of us is to be in a group where other members all have a shared knowledge from which we are excluded. This can all too easily be the experience of some of our pupils, through cultural or social disadvantage or because of learning difficulties of one sort or another.

Some of your pupils may live in families in which there is an emphasis on learning about and understanding the world around us. The family may talk, ask and answer questions, watch interesting TV programmes together, look at books, search the internet, go to the library, read newspapers, travel, go and visit local places of interest and so on, with the result that the children acquire a wealth of information. They will have confidence and a sense of belonging to the society in which they live. Not only this, very often their curiosity is nurtured and they will continue to discover how much in our world is intriguing, interesting or astounding.

Other pupils may come from homes where there is a restricted interest in the wider world and where the children's natural curiosity is dampened by lack of stimulation, or redirected to a limiting set of topics (such as celebrities, TV or film characters or commercial entertainment).

We must also not forget the pupils who experience learning difficulties in one form or another. For these pupils their narrower world may simply result from their difficulties in reading, understanding or thinking about the information that is all around them.

Many of the items in the following activities require active research by your pupils. In turn, this will help you to teach them strategies to find out the answers they need. This experience can have a far-reaching impact on pupils who have previously given up on questions for which the answers were not immediately evident.

Much general knowledge is learned implicitly rather than explicitly. Some of the following activities will give you, the teacher, the opportunity to fast-track your pupils' knowledge base of the world around them. One of the greatest benefits may be the way in which your pupils' curiosity is stimulated, with a positive spin-off across the curriculum.

Activity 15: All about animals

Teaching notes

All about animals is a fun activity to get all your pupils thinking and talking about animals! The questions can really stretch the pupils' knowledge and there may be times when everyone needs to check with a reference source to be sure they have the right answers.

You will notice that this is not an 'odd one out' activity. Instead, one, two or three of the suggested animals can fit the description. This is much, much harder than choosing the odd one out!

Level 1

1 **a** seagull **b** bat
2 **a** lion **c** seal
3 **c** goat
4 **a** porcupine **b** hedgehog
5 **a** frog **b** duck **c** goose
6 **b** squirrel
7 **a** human **b** monkey **c** parrot
8 **a** tiger
9 **a** hippopotamus **b** horse

Level 2

1 **a** tiger **c** zebra
2 **a** leopard **c** gorilla
3 **a** terrapin **c** snail
4 **a** wombat **b** rabbit **c** fox
5 **a** mouse **c** tortoise
6 **b** rattlesnake
7 **a** donkey **b** cow **c** sheep
8 **a** penguin
9 **c** orang-utan

Level 3

1 **b** hedgehog **c** bat
2 **a** ape **c** human
3 **c** sheep
4 **a** mongoose
5 **b** dodo **c** sabre-toothed tiger
6 **b** dolphin **c** porpoise
7 **b** locust **c** whale
8 **b** wolf **c** cheetah
9 **a** giraffe **b** cow **c** goat

Activity 15

All about animals

LEVEL 1

Answer these questions.

1 Which of these animals can fly?

    a seagull   **b** bat   **c** frog

2 Which of these animals have fur?

    a lion   **b** crocodile   **c** seal

3 Which of these animals have four legs?

    a emu   **b** caterpillar   **c** goat

4 Which of these animals have prickles?

    a porcupine   **b** hedgehog   **c** alligator

5 Which of these animals lay eggs?

    a frog   **b** duck   **c** goose

6 Which of these animals have long tails?

    a mole   **b** squirrel   **c** hare

7 Which of these animals sometimes eat fruit?

    a human   **b** monkey   **c** parrot

8 Which of these animals usually eat meat?

    a tiger   **b** camel   **c** chicken

9 Which of these animals eat grass?

    a hippopotamus   **b** horse   **c** hyena

Activity 15

All about animals

LEVEL 2

Answer these questions.

1 Which of these animals have striped coats?

   a tiger   **b** cheetah   **c** zebra

2 Which of these animals can climb trees?

   a leopard   **b** bear   **c** gorilla

3 Which of these animals have a shell?

   a terrapin   **b** dingo   **c** snail

4 Which of these animals sleep underground?

   a wombat   **b** rabbit   **c** fox

5 Which of these animals have a brain?

   a mouse   **b** worm   **c** tortoise

6 Which of these animals are poisonous?

   a boa constrictor   **b** rattlesnake   **c** python

7 Which of these animals have hooves?

   a donkey   **b** cow   **c** sheep

8 Which of these animals like salt water?

   a penguin   **b** frog   **c** beaver

9 Which of these animals make a nest to sleep in?

   a gazelle   **b** bear   **c** orang-utan

Activity 15

All about animals

LEVEL 3

Answer these questions.

1   Which of these animals hibernate?
    a rabbit   **b** hedgehog   **c** bat

2   Which of these animals are primates?
    a ape   **b** elephant   **c** human

3   Which of these animals never eat meat?
    a chimpanzee **b** cat   **c** sheep

4   Which of these animals are not marsupials?
    a mongoose   **b** koala   **c** kangaroo

5   Which of these animals are extinct?
    a puma   **b** dodo   **c** sabre-toothed tiger

6   Which of these animals are cetaceans?
    a shark   **b** dolphin   **c** porpoise

7   Which of these animals migrate?
    a kangaroo   **b** locust   **c** whale

8   Which of these animals are predators?
    a antelope   **b** wolf   **c** cheetah

9   Which of these animals are ruminants?
    a giraffe   **b** cow   **c** goat

From: *Spotlight on Your Inclusive Classroom*, Routledge © Glynis Hannell 2009

Activity 16: Do you know?

Teaching notes

Do you know? will get your pupils thinking! They will have to visualise, deduce, infer and draw on pre-existing knowledge. They may even have to guess! Some of the questions are closed with one definite answer, while others are open to discussion. Encourage your pupils to investigate more fully where appropriate, for example why milk goes sour or what paper is made from. There is a lot of science to be learned from some of these topics!

Below are the answers and some suggested discussion points.

Level 1

1   Four.

2   To keep it safe; to earn interest.

3   Right-handed.

4   Blossom.

5   Speed, distance, engine performance, etc.

6   It goes sour. (Discuss role of bacteria with your pupils.)

7   At the bottom, opposite the 12.

8   For unique identification, registration.

9   Usually inwards to prevent injury to callers.

Level 2

1   It should go off; there is a switch that operates as the door closes.

2   Electricity and telephone services. (Discuss that sometimes these are underground.)

3   No, as snow has more volume than water.

4   Petrol, milk, compressed gas, chemicals, etc.

5   Four; some dogs have a residual fifth toe called a 'dew claw'.

6   Through pipes, usually to a sewage works or maybe a septic tank.

7   A wind-up clock; a sundial.

8   Right.

9   Wood pulp, recycled paper, cotton, fibre such as straw, banana leaves, etc.

Level 3

1   It can be read by a machine and linked to a computer to give price, etc.

2   Fabrics may be woven or knitted. (Perhaps give your pupils scraps of fabric to unravel.)

3   Late afternoon when the sun is lower in the sky.

4   Television signals are sent to a satellite in space and then bounced back to the satellite dish on Earth.

5   Side to side.

6   There are two rows of teeth that fit together when the slider pulls them close.

7   Ground floor.

8   Police, fire and ambulance.

9   The water turns into water vapour and goes into the air.

Activity 16

Do you know?

LEVEL 1

Answer these questions.

1   How many prongs does a fork usually have?

2   Why do people keep money in a bank?

3   Are most people left-handed or right-handed?

4   Which comes first on an apple tree, blossom or fruit?

5   What do the displays on the car dashboard tell the driver?

6   What happens to milk when it is warm for a long while?

7   Where is the 6 on a clock face?

8   Why do cars have number plates?

9   Do front doors usually open outwards or inwards?

From: *Spotlight on Your Inclusive Classroom*, Routledge © Glynis Hannell 2009

Activity 16

Do you know?

LEVEL 2

Answer these questions.

1 Does the light in the fridge stay on all the time? If not how does it switch off?

2 You often see wires, supported by poles, high above the street. What are the wires for?

3 If a cupful of snow melts, will the cup be full of water?

4 You sometimes see large tankers on the road. What are they carrying?

5 How many toes does a dog have on each front foot?

6 When you flush the toilet, where does it all go?

7 What sort of clock can keep going without electricity?

8 If there are two taps, which one is usually for the cold water, left or right?

9 What is paper made from?

Activity 16

LEVEL 3

Do you know?

Answer these questions.

1 Most things you buy have a bar code on them. What is it for?

2 Look at the fabric in your clothes. Can you work out how it is made?

3 Are shadows longest at midday or late afternoon?

4 Why do people put satellite dishes on their roofs?

5 When a dog wags his tail does the tail go mostly up and down or mostly side to side?

6 How does a zipper work?

7 In a lift there are usually some buttons to press. What does 'G' stand for?

8 There are three types of emergency services. What are they?

9 If you put wet things outside in the sun to dry, where does the water go?

Activity 17: Sports

Teaching notes

Sport plays an important part in the community and knowing something about the vocabulary and rules helps all pupils to be included and participate. Many of these questions lend themselves to classroom brainstorming, where some pupils may have more specific knowledge than others. It all adds up to everyone learning something new! Sometimes there is a range of correct answers!

Level 1

1 Tennis ball.

2 Tennis, volley ball, table tennis.

3 Retrieves the ball after it has been hit.

4 A racquet.

5 Soccer, hockey, cricket, rugby.

6 Gold, silver and bronze.

7 Keeps order; starts and finishes the match.

8 Swimming.

9 Members of a team take turns to run, swim, etc.

Level 2

1 Soccer, basketball, hockey.

2 Seven.

3 Runners have to jump hurdles as well as run.

4 In the wrong position.

5 Every four years.

6 Eleven.

7 Swimming, cycling and running.

8 Competitors throw a javelin (a long stick with a sharp point).

9 No points.

Level 3

1 Fishing.

2 Skiing is on snow and uses skis; skating is on ice and uses skates.

3 An arena for track cycling.

4 26 miles 385 yards/42.195 kilometres.

5 Badminton.

6 A cycle race through France.

7 Skiing.

8 Eighteen.

9 Olympic Games for people with disabilities.

Activity 17

Sports

LEVEL 1

Answer these questions.

1   Which is the largest, a golf ball or a tennis ball?

2   In which sports does the ball have to go over a net?

3   What does a fielder do in cricket or baseball?

4   What is the bat used in tennis called?

5   Which sports are played on a pitch?

6   What colour medals are given for 1st, 2nd and 3rd places at the Olympic Games?

7   What does an umpire or referee do?

8   Which sport uses a butterfly stroke?

9   What happens in a relay race?

Activity 17

Sports

LEVEL 2

Answer these questions.

1 In which sport do the players dribble the ball?

2 How many players are there in a netball team?

3 What happens in a hurdles race?

4 What does 'offside' mean?

5 How often are the Olympic Games held?

6 How many players are there in a cricket team?

7 What are the three sports in a triathlon?

8 What happens in a javelin competition?

9 What does the score 'love' mean in tennis?

Activity 17

Sports

LEVEL 3

Answer these questions.

1   What is another name for angling?

2   What is the difference between skiing and skating?

3   What is a velodrome?

4   How far is a marathon race?

5   In which sport is a shuttlecock used?

6   What is the Tour de France?

7   In which sport is the word 'slalom' used?

8   How many holes are there on a golf course?

9   What are the Paralympics?

From: *Spotlight on Your Inclusive Classroom*, Routledge © Glynis Hannell 2009

Activity 18: Planet Earth

Teaching notes

We live on a wonderful planet called Earth, but many pupils see and think only about their own, local, manmade environment. *Planet Earth* offers an opportunity for you and your pupils to take a look at some basic geographical facts about the natural Earth, without any mention of man's influence or impact. This will especially benefit your pupils whose home environments do not encourage an awareness or interest in the natural world. There are many opportunities for building discussions around the following answers.

Level 1

1 **a** hardly any rain

2 **b** hotter

3 **a** in the hills or mountains

4 **c** ice

5 **c** shines on the other half of the Earth

6 **a** travels around the Earth

7 **b** has mountains and volcanoes

8 **b** there are very hot liquid rocks

9 **a** the third planet from the sun

Level 2

1 **a** cooler

2 **b** more water (65 per cent water, 35 per cent land)

3 **b** fresh water (formed from snow and ice in glaciers)

4 **b** lightning travels fastest

5 **c** parts of the Earth's crust moving against each other

6 **a** was made millions of years ago from plants

7 **c** plenty of water and sunshine

8 **a** it is hard to breathe because there is not much oxygen

9 **c** snow slides down a mountain

Level 3

1 **a** the sun does not set in the summertime

2 **c** a ring or chain of islands made of coral

3 **a** the tops of the trees

4 **b** mostly nitrogen (about 78 per cent)

5 **b** blue light rays are scattered more easily than red or yellow

6 **b** the wind and the waves gradually wear them away

7 **c** are made of carbon

8 **a** the eye

9 **b** rivers of ice moving slowly towards lower ground

Activity 18

Planet Earth

LEVEL 1

Choose the right phrase to finish these sentences.

1 A desert has _____
   a hardly any rain   **b** lots of rain   **c** lots of thunderstorms

2 If you dig very deep into the Earth the air is _____
   a cooler   **b** hotter   **c** the same as on the ground

3 Rivers usually start _____
   a in the hills or mountains   **b** in the sea   **c** in a waterfall

4 Hail is made of _____
   a rain   **b** snow   **c** ice

5 When the sun sets it _____
   a goes behind a hill   **b** goes under the ground
   c shines on the other half of the Earth

6 The moon _____
   a travels around the Earth   **b** travels around the sun
   c stays in the same spot

7 The bottom of the ocean _____
   a is flat and sandy like a beach   **b** has mountains and volcanoes
   c is unknown to humans

8 The Earth is like a big ball; in the middle _____
   a there is a hole like a big cave   **b** there are very hot liquid rocks
   c we don't know what there is

9 The Earth is _____
   a the third planet from the sun   **b** the nearest planet to the sun
   c the furthest planet from the sun

Activity 18

Planet Earth

Choose the right phrase to finish these sentences.

LEVEL 2

1 If you go up very high the air is _____
  a cooler **b** hotter **c** the same as on the ground

2 On the Earth's surface there is _____
  a more land **b** more water **c** the same amount of land and water

3 Icebergs are made of _____
  a seawater **b** fresh water **c** milk

4 In a thunderstorm it is true that _____
  a thunder travels fastest **b** lightning travels fastest
  c thunder and lightning travel at the same speed

5 Earthquakes are caused by _____
  a thunderstorms that shake the ground
  b underground explosions caused by oil and gas
  c parts of the Earth's crust moving against each other

6 Coal under the ground _____
  a was made millions of years ago from plants
  b was made by rocks getting squashed together
  c was made from the soot of cavemen's fires

7 Plants grow best when there is _____
  a plenty of water **b** plenty of sunshine **c** plenty of water and sunshine

8 At the top of the highest mountains _____
  a it is hard to breathe because there is not much oxygen
  b it is much hotter because you are nearer the sun
  c you are up in the clouds and it is hard to see anything

9 An avalanche is when _____
  a snow piles up against a house **b** a volcano erupts
  c snow slides down a mountain

Activity 18

Planet Earth

LEVEL 3

Choose the right phrase to finish these sentences.

1 At the North and South Poles _____
  a the sun does not set in the summertime
  b in winter it is never dark
  c there is half sunlight and half darkness all year round

2 An atoll is _____
  a an island covered in ice **b** an island made of huge rocks
  c a ring or chain of islands made of coral

3 The canopy in a rainforest is _____
  a the tops of the trees **b** the forest floor
  c the smaller plants that grow underneath the taller trees

4 The Earth's atmosphere contains _____
  a mostly carbon dioxide **b** mostly nitrogen **c** mostly oxygen

5 The sky looks blue because _____
  a air is blue and you can see it in the sky
  b blue light rays are scattered more easily than red or yellow
  c the blue sea is reflected in the sky

6 There are often cliffs at the coast and _____
  a they are so tough they stay the same forever
  b the wind and the waves gradually wear them away
  c they crumble away as soon as it rains

7 Diamonds are found deep in the Earth and _____
  a are made of a sort of glass **b** are made from dead sea
  creatures **c** are made of carbon

8 The centre of a hurricane is called _____
  a the eye **b** the storm surge **c** the typhoon

9 Glaciers are _____
  a sheets of ice covering a mountain
  b rivers of ice moving slowly towards lower ground
  c baby icebergs that break off from bigger ones

From: *Spotlight on Your Inclusive Classroom*, Routledge © Glynis Hannell 2009

Activity 19: Places and names

Teaching notes

Places and names is an activity that will get your pupils using reference resources, such as an atlas, a globe and the internet. The questions are certainly not ones that most pupils will be able to answer without researching, talking and sometimes guessing! Some pupils may come from homes where even the adults would lack basic geographical knowledge of this type.

An awareness of the world around them helps to provide your pupils with a context for learning and understanding across the curriculum and in the wider community.

Level 1

1 c an ocean

2 a the Amazon

3 c Everest

4 c a desert

5 a Africa

6 c China

7 a the Arctic

8 c an island

9 a Canada

Level 2

1 b in the Arctic

2 c Italian

3 c the Himalayas

4 a Vesuvius

5 a France

6 c the Mississippi

7 b in the Pacific Ocean, close to Australia

8 b in the Southern Hemisphere

9 a the Pacific and Atlantic Oceans

Level 3

1 a an imaginary line where the sun is overhead once a year

2 b the Arctic

3 c the Nile

4 b the equator

5 c the Atlantic

6 a the Andes

7 b Africa

8 b Greece

9 c India

Activity 19

Places and names

LEVEL 1

Choose the right answer to these questions.

1 Which would have the most water in it? _____
   a a sea **b** a lake **c** an ocean

2 Which one of these is a river? _____
   a the Amazon **b** the Alps **c** the North Sea

3 Which one of these is a mountain? _____
   a London **b** Paris **c** Everest

4 What is the Sahara? _____
   a a forest **b** a lake **c** a desert

5 On which continent do lions live in the wild? _____
   a Africa **b** Australia **c** America

6 Which of these countries is the biggest? _____
   a England **b** France **c** China

7 Where do polar bears live? _____
   a the Arctic **b** Denmark **c** Greenland

8 What is Hawaii? _____
   a a river **b** a mountain **c** an island

9 Which of these countries would be the coldest? _____
   a Canada **b** Spain **c** Mexico

Activity 19

Places and names

LEVEL 2

Choose the right answer to these questions.

1 Where is the North Pole? _____
   a on the equator   **b** in the Arctic   **c** in the Antarctic

2 Which one of these is not the name of an ocean? _____
   a Indian   **b** Pacific   **c** Italian

3 What is the highest mountain range in the world? _____
   a the Alps   **b** the Rockies   **c** the Himalayas

4 Which of these is the name of an active volcano? _____
   a Vesuvius   **b** Rocky Mountain   **c** Ben Nevis

5 Which one of these countries is in Europe? _____
   a France   **b** Canada   **c** Japan

6 Which of these rivers is in the United States of America?

   _____
   a the Nile   **b** the Murray   **c** the Mississippi

7 Where is the Great Barrier Reef? _____
   a in the Indian Ocean, close to India
   b in the Pacific Ocean, close to Australia
   c in the Atlantic Ocean, close to Jamaica

8 Where is Australia? _____
   a in the Northern Hemisphere   **b** in the Southern
   Hemisphere   **c** on the equator

9 Which oceans are connected by the Panama canal? _____
   a the Pacific and Atlantic Oceans
   b the Southern and Pacific Oceans
   c the Indian and Atlantic Oceans

Activity 19

Places and names

LEVEL 3

Choose the right answer to these questions.

1 What is the Tropic of Cancer? _____
   a an imaginary line where the sun is overhead once a year
   b an imaginary line that joins the North and South Poles
   c an imaginary line to show where it is always warm and sunny

2 Which one of these is not the name of a continent? _____
   a Australia   **b** the Arctic   **c** Antarctica

3 What is the longest river in the world? _____
   a the Congo   **b** the Mississippi   **c** the Nile

4 If you sailed from the Northern to the Southern Hemisphere, what would you cross? _____
   a the international dateline   **b** the equator
   c the northern lights

5 If you travelled from London to New York, which ocean would you cross? _____
   a the Indian   **b** the Pacific   **c** the Atlantic

6 What is the longest mountain range in the world? _____
   a the Andes   **b** the Rockies   **c** the Alps

7 On which continent would you find the Kalahari desert? _____
   a South America   **b** Africa   **c** Australia

8 Which of these countries has beaches on the Mediterranean Sea?
   _____
   a Sweden   **b** Greece   **c** Portugal

9 The Ganges is a river in which country? _____
   a China   **b** Egypt   **c** India

   From: *Spotlight on Your Inclusive Classroom*, Routledge © Glynis Hannell 2009

Activity 20: The human body

Teaching notes

As children develop they begin to learn more about *The human body* and how it works. As well as being intrinsically interesting, this understanding can be an important foundation for a healthy lifestyle. Encourage your pupils to use reference sources to find out the answers to the questions that they do not know right away.

Level 1

1 **b** your teeth

2 **a** into your stomach

3 **c** skull

4 **c** speed up

5 **a** to get as much air as you can

6 **b** your leg to your body

7 **b** get larger when it is dark

8 **a** get plenty of exercise

9 **c** to keep the germs away

Level 2

1 **a** something that pumps your blood around your body

2 **b** the palms of your hands

3 **b** your muscles pull your bones

4 **b** your ribs

5 **a** the iris

6 **c** inside your ear

7 **c** keep working, but in a different way from when you are awake

8 **b** we all have fingerprints and every single one is different

9 **b** people may have touched it with dirty hands before you bought it

Level 3

1 **c** only pull

2 **b** left side of brain controls right side of body; right side of brain controls left side of body

3 **c** you breathe in oxygen and breathe out carbon dioxide

4 **c** your bone marrow

5 **a** attack the germs that could make you ill

6 **c** children have more bones than adults (about 300 infant bones fuse into 206 adult bones)

7 **a** filter your blood and make urine

8 **b** helps you to breathe

9 **b** carries messages to and from your brain and the rest of your body

Activity 20

The human body

LEVEL 1

Choose the right answer to these questions.

1   Which part of your body cuts and grinds food? _____

    a your jawbones **b** your teeth **c** your fingers

2   After your food leaves your mouth, where does it go? _____

    a into your stomach **b** into your lungs **c** into your liver

3   What are the bones that protect your brain called? _____

    a brain bones **b** spine **c** skull

4   If you run very fast, what does your heart do? _____

    a beat slower **b** keep beating at the same speed **c** speed up

5   Why do you take a deep breath of air before you go underwater?

    _____

    a to get as much air as you can **b** to make yourself float like a
balloon **c** to stop the water getting into your mouth

6   What does your hip connect? _____

    a your head to your neck **b** your leg to your body
    c your foot to your leg

7   What do the pupils in your eyes do? _____

    a stay the same size all the time **b** get larger when it is dark
    c get smaller when it is dark

8   What should you do to help your bones to grow strong? _____

    a get plenty of exercise **b** rest your bones as much as you can
    c be careful not to fall over

9   Why do you put a bandage or plaster on a cut? _____

    a so it does not look yukky **b** to stop it hurting
    c to keep the germs away

Activity 20

The human body

LEVEL 2

Choose the right answer to these questions.

1 What is the best description of your heart? _____
   a something that pumps your blood around your body
   b something that warms up your blood when you are cold
   c something that cools down your blood when you are hot

2 Which part of your body does not have any hair on it? _____
   a your face   **b** the palms of your hands   **c** your legs

3 How are you able to run? _____
   a your joints move and make your bones move   **b** your muscles pull your bones   **c** your bones move by themselves

4 Which bones protect your lungs, liver and heart? _____
   a your pelvis   **b** your ribs   **c** your collarbones

5 What is the part of your eye that is coloured blue, brown, green or grey called? _____
   a the iris   **b** the cornea   **c** the pupil

6 Where is the smallest bone in your body? _____
   a inside your mouth   **b** inside your eye   **c** inside your ear

7 When you are asleep, what does your brain do? _____
   a switches off completely   **b** keeps going just the same as when you are awake   **c** keeps working, but in a different way from when you are awake

8 Which of these is true? _____
   a only criminals have fingerprints   **b** we all have fingerprints and every single one is different   **c** babies have exactly the same fingerprints as their mothers

9 Why should you always wash fruit and salad before you eat it?

   _____
   a it tastes better when it has been washed   **b** people may have touched it with dirty hands before you bought it   **c** washing keeps it fresh and crisp

Activity 20

The human body

Choose the right answer to these questions.   **LEVEL 3**

1   What can the muscles of the human body do? _____
     a push and pull   **b** only push   **c** only pull

2   The brain has two sides. Which of the following is correct? _____
     a left side of brain controls left side of body; right side of brain
     controls right side of body   **b** left side of brain controls right
     side of body; right side of brain controls left side of body
     c both sides of brain control both sides of body

3   What happens when you breathe? _____
     a you breathe in carbon dioxide and breathe out oxygen
     b you breathe in oxygen and breathe out nitrogen
     c you breathe in oxygen and breathe out carbon dioxide

4   Where are your red blood cells made? _____
     a your liver   **b** your heart   **c** your bone marrow

5   What do your white blood cells do? _____
     a attack the germs that could make you ill   **b** carry oxygen around
     your system   **c** help your blood to clot when you are hurt

6   Which is true? _____
     a adults and children have the same number of bones in their bodies
     b adults have more bones than children   **c** children have more
     bones than adults

7   What do your kidneys do? _____
     a filter your blood and make urine   **b** protect you from getting too
     cold   **c** help you to digest meat

8   What does your diaphragm do? _____
     a helps you to digest food   **b** helps you to breathe
     c helps you to balance

9   What does your spinal cord do? _____
     a keeps your back straight   **b** carries messages to and from your
     brain and the rest of your body   **c** stops the bones in your back
     from rubbing against each other

    From: *Spotlight on Your Inclusive Classroom*, Routledge © Glynis Hannell 2009

Activity 21: The right thing to do

Teaching notes

Knowing *The right thing to do* is an important part of learning about the world around us. Children who understand the ground rules of social interaction and decision making find it easier to fit into their peer group, family and community. These items are all about making good choices. Many pupils get into strife because they are not able to make sensible, responsible choices in the heat of the moment.

We know that using cognitive strategies to deal with potentially difficult situations usually produces the best outcomes, but this is not always easy. Many pupils lack experience in thinking out strategies to deal with the inevitable ups and downs that they will encounter at home, at school and in the community. Reactions are sometimes impulsive and increase, rather than decrease, the initial problem. For example, a pupil denies knocking over a smaller child; a long series of excuses is fabricated to explain lost homework; bullying is ignored; and small emergencies produce panic.

The right thing to do is best done as a series of classroom discussions, in which all pupils can contribute their thoughts and suggestions. This helps pupils of varying abilities to collaborate and learn from each other and learn more about the options they have to deal with some of life's tricky problems.

Teachers will notice that some pupils will need the questions to be read aloud. It is important to do this where necessary so that all pupils can participate equally.

As you discuss the items take the opportunity to talk to your pupils about the value of personal qualities, such as:

- being honest;

- being courageous where necessary;

- showing kindness, especially to those weaker, younger or less well-off than yourself;

- playing fair;

- using common sense;

- being resourceful and using initiative;

- being courteous;

- taking responsibility for your own actions;

- seeking adult help when appropriate.

Activity 21

The right thing to do

LEVEL 1

What is the right thing to do if . . .?

1   you accidentally knock a small child over

2   you find a friend's toy in your school bag

3   you are lost in a large shop

4   you see a baby all alone in the street

5   you cannot remember what homework the teacher told you to do

6   there is a very fierce dog in the playground

7   you got really mad and shouted at the teacher

8   a little kid at school tries to fight you

9   you find some yummy biscuits in the playground

Activity 21

The right thing to do

LEVEL 2

What is the right thing to do if . . .?

1 you see your neighbour's house on fire

2 your grandma is looking after you, but suddenly she gets very sick

3 you are at a neighbour's house, but you do not feel safe

4 you lost your homework and the teacher is asking for it

5 your friend has forgotten his school lunch

6 you see an old man kicked and robbed by someone who runs away

7 the other kids are mean to you and won't let you play with them

8 you see one of the younger kids being bullied by a big kid

9 a shopkeeper has given you too much change

Activity 21

The right thing to do

LEVEL 3

What is the right thing to do if . . .?

1 you see an old lady trying to get her shopping trolley up a steep slope

2 you get an email or text that says horrible things about another kid

3 you go home by bus, but you miss your stop

4 some older kids ask you to help them steal another kid's lunch

5 someone you know though the internet wants to meet you

6 your best friend wants you to ignore another friend

7 you belong to the soccer team, but you don't feel like going to team practice

8 a car crash happens right outside your house

9 you've just promised to go to Jack's house, but forgot that you had already promised to help Dad with the chores at home

CHAPTER 5

Puzzles and riddles

Learning can be fun!

The Spotlight series of books provides teachers with a wide range of activities to promote pupils' learning in an inclusive, interactive classroom. In this final chapter of *Spotlight on Your Inclusive Classroom* it is time for some fun as well as a continuation of some serious learning.

The ability to use clues and work with a scaffold of information is important in many types of learning, and relies on the pupils' willingness to make a guess and put together information from two or more sources. *Vowel animals* (Activity 22) and *Help!* (Activity 26) both provide clues, but then let pupils work things out for themselves. *Vowel animals* does promote spelling skills, whereas *Help!* is more open-ended and allows pupils to be creative with their own ideas.

This chapter also contains some well-loved, traditional *Jokes* and *Riddles* (Activities 23 and 24). Look carefully at them and you will see that they also offer some very useful teaching opportunities. For example, words such as *moosic* or *oinkment* are fun wordplays that involve phonological twists and puns.

The *Riddles* are a very interesting set of questions for the teacher to look at. Notice how often the pupils will be caught out if they do not listen carefully. *Tim has 8 apples and you take away 2. How many do you have?* is typical. Many pupils will instinctively say 6, even though, if you listen carefully, the question asks *how many you have* (the correct answer, of course, is 2). Often the riddles make pupils think carefully and to succeed they will need to ignore the 'red herrings'. Look at this one, for example. *Tom's father had four sons. The three oldest boys were called Monday, Tuesday and Wednesday. What was the youngest son called?* How many of your pupils will fall for the trap of following on the sequence of names and think that the last son is called Thursday? (the correct answer of course is *Tom*).

Acronyms (Activity 25) are commonly used in everyday life, but sometimes they can be as hard as riddles for pupils to understand. This activity gives your pupils a chance to come to terms with acronyms that they will encounter, while *Help!* (Activity 26) lets your pupils use their imaginations to work out what invented acronyms might stand for.

Last, but not least, *How many things?* (Activity 27) is a word-finding activity where pupils can work together to see how many things they can think of to meet the descriptions. It's harder than it looks!

Activity 22: Vowel animals

Teaching notes

In this activity pupils have to think of animal names. They are given a clue and the vowels of the name to help them. This stretches thinking, phonological and spelling skills. The pupils will have to integrate several types of information to arrive at the correct solutions. Groups work best as pupils can support each other and work things out together.

Level 1

1 dog

2 pig

3 cat

4 duck

5 frog

6 sheep

7 lion

8 rabbit

9 goat

Level 2

1 horse

2 elephant

3 monkey

4 whale

5 hippopotamus

6 alligator

7 parrot

8 tortoise

9 kitten

Level 3

1 polar bear

2 iguana

3 cheetah

4 baboon

5 hedgehog

6 kangaroo

7 panda

8 penguin

9 squirrel

Activity 22

LEVEL 1

Vowel animals

Fill in the letters to complete the animal names.

	Animal	Clue
1	_ o _	I like to go for walks.
2	_ i _	I say 'oink'.
3	_ a _	I like to drink milk.
4	_ u _ _	I have feathers and I can swim.
5	_ _ o _	I can jump and I can swim.
6	_ _ e e _	I have a thick fleece.
7	_ i o _	I like to hunt and then sleep in the sun.
8	_ a _ _ i _	I am a pet, but I often live outdoors.
9	_ o a _	I am not a cow, but I give milk.

Activity 22

Vowel animals

Fill in the letters to complete the animal names.

	Animal	Clue
1	_ o _ _ e	You can ride me.
2	e _ e _ _ a _ _	You can ride me, too, and I have big ears.
3	_ o _ _ e _	I am related to you!
4	_ _ a _ e	I live in the sea and I am huge.
5	_ i _ _ o _ o _ a _ u _	I live in the rivers in Africa.
6	a _ _ i _ a _ o _	Watch out! I have sharp teeth.
7	_ a _ _ o _	I might copy what you say.
8	_ o _ _ o i _ e	I have a shell, but I am not a snail.
9	_ i _ _ e _	I like to play. I am only a baby.

Activity 22

Vowel animals

LEVEL 3

Fill in the letters to complete the animal names.

Animal	Clue
1 _ o _ a _ _ e a _	I am white and I catch fish to eat (2 words).
2 i _ u a _ a	I am a reptile.
3 _ _ e e _ a _	I am a big cat and I run very fast.
4 _ a _ o o _	I am a member of the ape family.
5 _ e _ _ e _ o _	I curl up in a ball when I am scared.
6 _ a _ _ a _ o o	I am a marsupial, with a pouch.
7 _ a _ _ a	I am black and white.
8 _ e _ _ u i _	I am black and white, too.
9 _ _ _ i _ _ e _	I live in the trees and I sleep in a dray.

Activity 23: Jokes

Teaching notes

This *Jokes* activity is a really good way of expanding your pupils' thinking skills. Jokes challenge pupils to think laterally, to deal with the unexpected and to play with words and ideas. Jokes may involve a ridiculous application of logic, unexpected shifts in meaning and puns and tricks with words.

Many younger or less able pupils may need the teacher's help to understand some of the jokes. Discussion about why a joke was funny and how it 'worked' can prove to be a very useful activity for engaging pupils in thinking about words, concepts and logic! This type of discussion can also stimulate pupils to think about their own thinking (*metacognition*), which is a very important stepping stone in intellectual development.

Level 1

1   Snap.

2   Hide in a bucket.

3   Time to get a new fence.

4   Oinkment.

5   It saw the milk shake.

6   Because their horns don't work.

7   When they hear the moosic.

8   An ant's dinner.

9   Hop on.

Level 2

1   It wanted to play squash.

2   I'll be back in an hour.

3   His yellow ones were dirty.

4   The feather forecast.

5   Sir.

6   When it's going cheep.

7   When it's being toad.

8   Because it had the tweetment.

9   Traffic jam.

Level 3

1   About two miles an hour.

2   He had no body to go with.

3   Wrong.

4   He-never-saw-us rex.

5   It's too far to walk.

6   A little bear.

7   He didn't give a hoot.

8   I'm paw.

9   An udder failure.

Activity 23

Jokes

LEVEL 1

It's time to have some fun! Can you guess
the answers?

1   What is a crocodile's favourite game?

2   What can a rabbit do that an elephant can't do?

3   What is the time when the elephant sits on the
fence?

4   What do you give a sick pig?

5   Why did the jelly wobble?

6   Why do cows wear bells?

7   When do cows start to dance?

8   What is smaller than an ant's mouth?

9   What did the bus driver say to the frog?

Activity 23

Jokes

LEVEL 2

It's time to have some fun! Can you guess
the answers?

1 Why did the lemon stop in the middle of the
road?

2 What did the big hand say to the little hand?

3 Why did the elephant wear red pyjamas to bed?

4 What is a duck's favourite TV programme?

5 What do you call a gorilla in a rage?

6 When is the best time to buy a budgerigar?

7 When is a car like a frog?

8 Why did the bird feel better?

9 What do policemen put on their toast?

Activity 23

Jokes

LEVEL 3

It's time to have some fun! Can you guess
the answers?

1 What was the turtle doing on the motorway?

2 Why didn't the skeleton go to the party?

3 Which word in the dictionary is always spelled
wrong?

4 What do you call a dinosaur in a cave?

5 Why do swallows fly north in the spring?

6 What animal do you look like in the bath?

7 How did the owl feel when he had a sore
throat?

8 What did the cat say when she lost all her
money?

9 What did the farmer call the cow who did not
give any milk?

Activity 24: Riddles

Teaching notes

These *Riddles* are brain teasers to get all your pupils thinking. Lateral thinking, careful listening and imagination are needed to solve these riddles. Some of them are very old, traditional ones that have been around for generations. They still hold a fascination for today's pupils, who will enjoy finding out the quirky and sometimes nonsensical answers for themselves and then trying the riddles out on family and friends. It's all part of learning and belonging to a community.

Level 1

1 an egg

2 a pencil, a piece of soap

3 a doughnut, a rubber ring

4 stairs

5 a horse

6 a table, a chair

7 a dry stone

8 a bucket of water

9 lunch and dinner

Level 2

1 water, a river

2 it sinks

3 the letter 'e'

4 your age

5 time

6 they weigh the same, a kilo

7 a cold, measles

8 an onion

9 a hole

Level 3

1 Tom

2 a hole

3 covering sheep

4 two

5 breath

6 halfway in

7 Mount Everest

8 she is your mother

9 he lives in Australia

Activity 24

Riddles

LEVEL 1

See if you can solve these riddles.

1   What has to be broken before it can be used?

2   What is bigger when it is new, but gets smaller when it is old?

3   What has no middle, no beginning and no end?

4   What goes up and down without moving?

5   Which animal goes to sleep with its shoes on?

6   What has four legs but cannot walk?

7   What sort of stone is never found in the ocean?

8   What does not get any wetter, even if you leave it out in the rain for a whole day?

9   What are the two things you can never eat for breakfast?

Activity 24

Riddles

LEVEL 2

See if you can solve these riddles.

1   What runs but can never walk?

2   What happens when you throw a black rock into clear water?

3   What do you see twice in a week, once in a year, but never in a day?

4   What goes up and never comes down?

5   What flies without wings?

6   What weighs more, a kilo of pebbles or a kilo of bubbles?

7   What can you catch but never throw?

8   If you cut me, I won't cry, but you might.

9   What grows bigger and bigger the more you take away?

From: *Spotlight on Your Inclusive Classroom*, Routledge © Glynis Hannell 2009

Activity 24

Riddles

LEVEL 3

See if you can solve these riddles.

1   Tom's father had four sons. The three oldest
    boys were called Monday, Tuesday and
    Wednesday. What was the youngest son called?

2   What weighs nothing and cannot be seen but, if
    you put it into a box, will make the box lighter?

3   What is the world's greatest use for sheepskin?

4   Tim has eight apples and you take away two.
    How many do you have?

5   What is as light as a feather, but even the
    strongest man cannot hold it for long?

6   How far can you walk into a forest?

7   Before Mount Everest was discovered, what was
    the highest mountain in the world?

8   How could all your cousins have an aunt that is
    not your aunt?

9   Bruce's birthday is on 1 January. He always has
    his birthday in the summer. How does he do
    this?

Activity 25: Acronyms

Teaching notes

Acronyms occur quite often in everyday conversation, so it is useful for pupils to be aware of what the letters actually stand for. The activity may also stimulate your pupils' curiosity about other acronyms that they may come across.

There is room on the worksheets for your pupils to note what they think each acronym means, even if they do not know what the letters stand for. Some acronyms are self-evident, but others may not be so obvious. For example, *SOS*, *CCTV* or *UFO* may be quite familiar to your pupils even though they do not know what the letters stand for.

Some acronyms may have more than one meaning, but the most commonly used ones are given here.

Level 1

1 television

2 barbecue

3 save our souls

4 three-dimensional

5 United States of America

6 identification

7 United Kingdom

8 compact disc

9 orange juice

Level 2

1 very important person

2 world wide web

3 tender loving care

4 unidentified flying object

5 question and answer

6 as soon as possible

7 headquarters

8 closed-circuit television

9 disc jockey

Level 3

1 rest in peace

2 frequently asked question

3 personal computer

4 intelligence quotient

5 self-contained underwater breathing apparatus

6 répondez s'il vous plaît (please reply)

7 or near offer

8 also known as

9 World War 1

Activity 25

Acronyms

LEVEL 1

What do these letters stand for? What do they mean?

Acronym	What do the letters stand for?	What do they mean?
1 TV		
2 BBQ		
3 SOS		
4 3D		
5 USA		
6 ID		
7 UK		
8 CD		
9 OJ		

Activity 25

Acronyms

LEVEL 2

What do these letters stand for? What do they mean?

Acronym	What do the letters stand for?	What do they mean?
1 VIP		
2 WWW		
3 TLC		
4 UFO		
5 Q&A		
6 ASAP		
7 HQ		
8 CCTV		
9 DJ		

Activity 25

Acronyms

LEVEL 3

What do these letters stand for? What do they mean?

Acronym	What do the letters stand for?	What do they mean?
1 RIP		
2 FAQ		
3 PC		
4 IQ		
5 SCUBA		
6 RSVP		
7 ONO		
8 AKA		
9 WW1		

Activity 26: Help!

Teaching notes

In *Help!* your pupils have to use logic, word knowledge and imagination to work out what the acronyms might stand for. At the easier levels, the acronyms have a close link with the clues, but as the items get harder the links become less obvious, stretching your pupils' vocabularies and creativity. Of course, there are no 'right' answers, but your pupils will have fun making up plausible names to match the acronyms.

Pupils will need reminding that very small words such as *of*, *for* or *and* do not necessarily need a letter of their own. So, for example, with item 2 in Level 2, *Harry's Home for Dogs of Harrow* would be an acceptable solution for HHDH.

The following are possible solutions, but there are many more.

Level 1

1 Peanut Butter Super Sandwich; Pumpkin Bread Super Sandwich

2 Cheese and Tomato Super Sandwich; Chicken Tikka Super Sandwich

3 Jenny's Fresh Eggs

4 Dry Feet Boots

5 Very Quick Train

6 Brighton Girls' Netball Team

7 Chocolate Milk Shake; Coffee Milk Shake

8 Boys' Club; Basketball Competition

9 Do Not Drop; Deliver Next Door

Level 2

1 Please See Me; Poor Sam, Messy

2 Harry's Home for Desperate Hounds

3 Little Kids Play Park; Lively Kids Play Place

4 Magic Minute Machine

5 Portsmouth Ladies Aqua Club

6 Very Amazing Robot

7 Swindon Soccer Fan Club

8 Waste Paper Bags

9 Mersey Citizens

Level 3

1 Tenby Angling Club

2 Solar-Powered Grass Cutter

3 Amateur Athletics

4 Don't Know What

5 Ray's Shiny Window Service

6 Agricultural Equipment Store

7 Sam's Centre for Silver

8 Reading Hospital Emergency Department

9 International Travellers' Association

Activity 26

Help!

LEVEL 1

What could the letters stand for? Write down as many answers as you can think of.

1   The Super Sandwich Cafe only uses letters on the menu. John has a PBSS.

2   The Super Sandwich Cafe only uses letters on the menu. Jenna has a CTSS.

3   JFE is printed on the egg box.

4   Jack's new rubber boots have the letters DFB on them.

5   The train is very fast; it is called the VQT.

6   Jane plays netball with the BGNT.

7   There are lots of different milkshakes at the stall in the shopping mall. Frankie's favourite is a CMS.

8   The school has started a BC.

9   The label on the parcel says DND.

Activity 26

Help!

LEVEL 2

What could the letters stand for? Write down as many answers as you can think of.

1   The teacher wants to talk to Sam about his work. She puts PSM on his page.

2   Harry runs a home for stray dogs. The home is called the HHDH.

3   At the beach there is a play area for children under five years of age. The play area is called the LKPP.

4   The MMM is a machine that makes time go faster.

5   The club is called the PLAC.

6   The children have a toy that is called the VAR.

7   All the members of the SSFC went to watch their team play.

8   The shop had a notice saying <u>PUT YOUR WPB HERE</u>.

9   In the car park there was a notice saying <u>MC ONLY</u>.

From: *Spotlight on Your Inclusive Classroom*, Routledge © Glynis Hannell 2009

Activity 26

Help!

LEVEL 3

What could the letters stand for? Write down as many answers as you can think of.

1 Dad goes fishing with the TAC.

2 Harry has invented a lawnmower that uses the sun's energy. He calls it the SPGC.

3 Sally is in the AA's running team.

4 Mike sorts his photos out. He puts some of them in his DKW folder.

5 A window cleaning service is called RSWS.

6 The AES sells tractors and other equipment to farmers.

7 Sam sells silver knives and forks. His shop is called the SCS.

8 Ambulances take accident victims to the RHED.

9 The teacher went all over the world to visit other ITA members.

Activity 27: How many things?

Teaching notes

In *How many things?* the pupils have to think of as many things as they can that share a characteristic (such as coldness) or a function (such as transmitting messages). This is not always as easy as it sounds! The teacher will often find that discussion is needed to clarify the answers. *Will a bottle always float? No, only if it is empty. Is it true that glass will never bend? If so, how do they make bottles?*

The following are possible answers, but there are many more.

Level 1

1 stairs, ladder, swing, aircraft, lift . . .

2 bird, human, ape . . .

3 ice, snow, frost, hail, glacier, iceberg . . .

4 blood, tomato sauce, ruby, strawberry . . .

5 sugar, honey, fruit, chocolate . . .

6 ice, grease, silk, mud . . .

7 umbrella, roof, coat . . .

8 wood, cork, empty bottle . . .

9 penguin, zebra, zebra crossing . . .

Level 2

1 broom, hairbrush, hedgehog, porcupine . . .

2 wool, fur, fire, hot water bottle, sun . . .

3 hands, eyes, twins, shoes, feet, socks . . .

4 teapot, oil can, watering can . . .

5 river, sea, ocean, tears, rain . . .

6 telescope, zoom lens . . .

7 coal, gold, silver, diamonds, oil, gas . . .

8 aircraft, space rocket, hot-air balloon, satellite . . .

9 balanced diet, fresh air, exercise, sleep, vaccinations . . .

Level 3

1 collar, lead, fence, command . . .

2 peas, pages of a book, bees in a hive, raindrops in a storm . . .

3 flour, popcorn, mustard . . .

4 telephone, radio, voice, written word . . .

5 gold, diamonds, vegetables . . .

6 pebble, water . . .

7 stone, diamond, ice . . .

8 people in history, dinosaurs, other galaxies . . .

9 the oceans, the sun, the stars . . .

Activity 27

How many things

LEVEL 1

How many things can you think of that . . .?

1 help you go high

2 have two legs

3 are always cold

4 are always red

5 taste sweet

6 are slippery

7 keep you dry

8 will float

9 are always black and white

Activity 27

How many things

LEVEL 2

How many things can you think of that . . .?

1 have bristles

2 keep you warm

3 always come in pairs

4 have spouts

5 are always wet

6 help you see in the distance

7 are found underground

8 can go above the clouds

9 help you to keep healthy

Activity 27

How many things

LEVEL 3

How many things can you think of that . . .?

1   help to keep dogs under control

2   are always in groups of more than ten

3   are made from seeds

4   transmit messages

5   might have come from Africa

6   will never burn

7   will never bend

8   you could never see

9   will last for a million years